TRIAL AND ERROR

TRIAL AND ERROR

The American Civil Liberties Union and Its Impact on Your Family

George Grant

Wolgemuth & Hyatt, Publishers, Inc.
Brentwood, Tennessee

The mission of Wolgemuth & Hyatt, Publishers, Inc. is to publish and distribute books that lead individuals toward:

- A personal faith in the one true God: Father, Son, and Holy Spirit;

- A lifestyle of practical discipleship; and

- A worldview that is consistent with the historic, Christian faith.

Moreover, the Company endeavors to accomplish this mission at a reasonable profit and in a manner which glorifies God and serves His Kingdom.

Unless otherwise noted, all scripture quotations are either the author's own or are from the New King James Version of the Bible, © 1979, 1980, 1982, 1984 by Thomas Nelson, Inc., Nasville, Tennessee and are used by permission.

Wolgemuth & Hyatt, Publishers, Inc.
1749 Mallory Lane, Suite 110, Brentwood, Tennessee 37027.
Printed in the United States of America.

Library of Congress Cataloging-in-Publication Data

Grant, George, 1954-
    Trial and error : the American Civil Liberties Union and its impact on your family / George Grant. — 1st ed.
    p. cm.
    Includes bibliographical references.
    1. American Civil Liberties Union. 2. Civil rights
— Religious aspects — Christianity. 3. Political
rights — Religious aspects — Christianity. I. Title.
JC599.U5G687 1989   323'.06'073   89-24838
ISBN 0-943497-66-3

To Chester Belloc
who has never failed to serve me with
"a nasty dose of orthodoxy."

And to Karen Blake
who has never failed to serve me with
"a healthy dose of reality."

Exaltavit Humiles

CONTENTS

ACKNOWLEDGEMENTS

A ll writing is hard," says Paul Johnson. And, "creative writing is intellectual drudgery of the hardest kind."[1] That is why writers are so dependent upon the kindness of others.

In this regard, I am by no means exempt. In fact, during the months when I was researching and writing this book, it was only the kindness of others that kept me going. For this, I am extremely grateful.

Jim Braden of the Rutherford Institute, Gary DeMar of American Vision, and Doug Kay of Focus on the Family all provided me with much needed counsel, contacts, and resources.

The previously published work of a number of pioneering authors and researchers has also proven to be a tremendous help to me in tracking down obscure details and verifying odd citations. Heritage Foundation scholar, William Donohue, probably knows more about the ACLU than anyone alive, and thus, I have unashamedly relied on the wisdom, objectivity, and integrity of his work.[2] I have also looked to the work of John Whitehead, Bill McIlhany, Peggy Lamson, Daniel Dreisbach, Herb Titus, John Eidsmoe, Gary Amos, Paul Murphy, Ed Rowe, Patrick Buchanan, Phyllis Schlafly, Reed Irvine, Phoebe Courtney, Nat Hentoff, Aaron Wildavasky, Tim LaHaye, Joseph Bishop, Robert W. Lee, Richard and Susan Vigilante, Marvin Olasky, and Richard Delgaudio.[3]

My grammatical abilities can best be summarized by my motto: "I've never met a comma I could trust." For that reason, I am extremely grateful to and eternally dependent on my long-time administrative assistants Kathe Salazar and Mac N. Tosh, as well as the editorial wizards at Wolgemuth and Hyatt led by the intrepid Russ Sorensen.

Not only am I not a grammarian, I am not a lawyer. Thus, I greatly appreciate the legal counsel afforded this project by Jim Turner, a devoted public servant and a man of the highest Christian integrity — rare virtues indeed.

Several friends have supported and encouraged me throughout the process of pulling this material into a cohesive text: Matt and Nancy Roberts, Jerry and Margaret Wright, David and Debbie Dunham, Bruce and Joann Tippery, Jerry and Ande Stapella, Roger and Gladys Israels, Don and Suzanne Martin, Randy and Cindy Terry, David and Dolly Thoburn, Howard and Roberta Ahmanson, Jim and Brenda Jordan, Bob and Lynn Dwelle, Bill and Connie Marshner, Gary and Sharon North, David and Cheri Shepherd, and Ray and Karen Plevyak. To each of these yokefellows I owe a debt of gratitude that I can never hope to repay.

Skip Ewing, Ted Sandquist, Bob Bennett, Kemper Crabb, George Winston, and Michael Card smoothed the rough edges of the long tedious hours of writing by providing the soundtrack, while Mario Vargas Llosa, Hernando De Soto, A.N. Wilson, Peter Ackroyd, LeRoy Snell, and Gene Wolfe provided the midnight musings. Thanks for keeping on keeping on; your art is all heart.

Finally, my family stood behind me every step along the way spurring me on. Joel, Joanna, and Jesse yielded up precious family time "to let Dad work." And Karen once again suffered the indignities of temporary "publishing widowhood" with valor and Christian charity. Clearly, my family is a commonwealth of approbation: "My mind grows green again with your dew; for it is a second Nisan come, whose flowers serve as offerings, garlanded in all kinds of wreathes, laid at my door. Blessed is the cloud which has distilled in me its moisture."[4]

Feast of Patrick
Crockett, Texas

INTRODUCTION

divinum quiddam in morbo[1]

To introduce a book supposes the greatest difficulty — because of the inevitable, inescapable presupposing.[2]

Hilaire Belloc

A cloud was on the mind of men and wailing went the weather, yea, a sick cloud upon the soul when we were boys together. Science announced nonentity and art admired decay.[3]

G.K. Chesterton

S ince its founding at the beginning of this century, the American Civil Liberties Union — best known by its popular acronym: the ACLU — has been the center of a storm of controversy. Through its policy pronouncements, legal initiatives, educational programs, and political lobbying, the organization has thrust itself onto our culture's center stage through a dramatic transformation of our judicial and societal ecologies.

This short study is a cursory exploration of that cultural dynamic. Thus, it contains an abbreviated analysis of all those policies, legal actions, educational efforts, and lobbying activities. The book's primary emphasis, however, is on the philosophical underpinnings and mainsprings of the organization. In other words, I have tried to discover — and then report —

1

what the ACLU *is* and what it *believes* rather than simply what it *says* or *does*. I wanted to get to the root of the controversy over the ACLU not merely reiterate its salient points. I wanted to effectively and accurately portray the long-term impact of the organization on our society—on our individual families and on our nation—by uncovering its deepest and dearest intentions.

But as important as these various tasks may be (see Ephesians 5:11), I knew that I couldn't just stop there. And so, the book goes on to briefly propose solid Biblical *solutions* to the problems and dilemmas raised by the ACLU—as well as the American legal system that it has effectively recreated in its own image. I have outlined a possible *agenda* for positively reclaiming our schools, courts, and communities. Thus, I have attempted to shape the book so that it also can serve as a practical *tool* in the hands of faithful men and women—a *tool* to help them effect those *solutions* and that *agenda*.

≈ ≈ ≈

In most respects, the plan of this study is fairly straightforward.[4]

Part One provides a basic introduction to the important issues and personalities that have made the ACLU so controversial. Chapter One is a series of vignettes that profile the effects of the ACLU's activities on ordinary families and communities. Chapter Two simply explains what the ACLU is, how it operates, and why it is important to the questions of law and liberty in our day.

Part Two provides some of the essential organizational and historical facts of the ACLU. Chapter Three profiles its public relations rhetoric as well as its policy positions. Chapter Four outlines its history—including a brief biographical sketch of its founder, Roger Baldwin.

Part Three is the real "meat and potatoes" section of the book—outlining just where the ACLU stands on a number of vital issues. In Chapter Five the organization's position on religious freedom is examined. In Chapter Six the issues of life and death—abortion, infanticide, suicide, and euthanasia—are taken up. Chapter Seven deals with pornography, homosexuality, and other forms of deviant moral behavior. Finally, Chapter Eight covers the ACLU's policies on crime and punishment.

Part Four concludes the study with a development of Biblical strategies and agendas for the future. Chapter Nine demonstrates the crucial importance of philosophical presuppositions to everyday life. And Chapter Ten outlines the lifestyle patterns necessary to enact those presuppositions effectively.

Several appendices round out the work so that once the reader has come to the end of the book, he doesn't have to come to the end of his concern. Appendix A is a shopping list of action items: practical ways that we can begin to put into practice the principles outlined in the book. Appendix B is a summary of the facts surrounding the ACLU. It is suitable for reuse in study groups, Sunday School classes, neighborhood meetings, party caucuses, Bible studies, or issues awareness committees in the community. Appendix C is a list of organizational resources while Appendix D is a list of bibliographic resources. These are provided so that the reader can go on to a deeper and more specialized study of the issues raised in this small book.

ે৯ ે৯ ે৯

John Frame, one of America's foremost theologians, has rightly observed that, "belief in Biblical authority does not make everything simple."[5] But, it does make everything *possible* (see Philippians 4:13). There is no magic wand. But there is a way to resolve the grave issues raised in the American legal system by the ACLU and its various proponents and opponents.

As one small step toward that end, this book is humbly offered.

Deo Soli Gloria. Jesu Juva.

PART ONE

THE CRISIS

As always happens to miraculous things, the virtue has all gone out with the lapse of time.[1]

Hilaire Belloc

An imbecile habit has arisen in modern controversy of saying that such and such a creed can be held in one age but cannot be held in another. Some dogma, we are told, was credible in the twelfth century, but is not credible in the twentieth. You might as well say that a certain philosophy can be believed on Mondays, but cannot be believed on Tuesdays. You might as well say of a view of the cosmos that it was suitable to half-past three, but not suitable for half-past four. What a man can believe depends upon his philosophy, not upon the clock or the century.[2]

G.K. Chesterton

1

NIGHTMARE
ON MAIN STREET

sed tu contra audentior ito[3]

A good battle for justice is the beginning of all great songs.[4]
Hilaire Belloc

*It is absurd to say that you are especially advancing freedom
when you only use free thought to destroy free will.*[5]
G.K. Chesterton

M ike Ruestik had only been on the job as manager of a
small convenience store for two weeks when he ran
into his first major problem. It was a tough ethical problem
that became an even tougher legal problem.

A sales representative from the news and periodicals distributor that the store bought its inventory from was telling
Mike about a number of new products that the company was
offering to its customers — including a number of pornographic magazines. Mike wasn't interested. He placed his regular order of family-oriented magazines and comics and let it
go at that.

If only that had been the end of it.

Two days later, Mike received a very distressing call from a local lawyer. He was told that his "arbitrary refusal" to order certain magazines was "in effect censorship"—a "clear violation" of the free speech rights guaranteed by the First Amendment of the Constitution. He was then given an ultimatum: either stock the pornography in the store or face a lawsuit—a lawsuit that would almost certainly cost him his store and his livelihood.

"I couldn't believe this was happening to me," Mike said. "I asked the guy why I couldn't stock whatever I *wanted* to stock in my store. I asked him whatever happened to free enterprise and all that. I asked him why *my* First Amendment rights weren't being considered."

Apparently, the lawyer wasn't interested in hearing Mike's perspective on the issue. "It was like he wasn't even listening. All he cared about were those magazines. Well, I'm sorry. I'm trying to run a family business here, and I don't want that trash in my store. I told him I'd see him in court."

It never came to that. The corporate office decided not to litigate, and Mike was fired.[6]

* * *

Laurie MacLaughlin was just sixteen-years-old when she died. Her mother still has a hard time talking about it. A tortured combination of grief and rage furrows her brow when she tries.

It was very early in the morning on New Years Day when the tragic accident occurred. Laurie was driving home after baby-sitting for several families in her church that had gotten together for the evening. The pickup truck that broadsided her crossed over the median strip at nearly eighty-five miles an hour. The driver was drunk. Laurie was killed instantly.

The week before, the state's Department of Public Safety, in conjunction with the local police, had announced that it would be setting up sobriety check-points all along major traffic thoroughfares in an effort to cut down on the number of drunk driving accidents during the holidays. One of those check-points was to have been just two blocks from where Laurie was killed. But the state was never allowed to implement its plan.

Several public advocacy attorneys, arguing that the plan "flagrantly violated" the Fourth Amendment's prohibition on "unreasonable search and seizures," obtained a temporary restraining order to stop it. Their action, they later explained to reporters, was necessary in order to "protect the liberties of the citizens of this state from arbitrary, capricious, and unbridled police intrusion."

Tell that to Laurie MacLaughlin's mother.

"My daughter would be alive today," she said, "if only the police had been allowed to do their job. Since when is it illegal to enforce the law? Since when does exposing our communities to sheer license, protect the liberties of the citizens of this state?"

Indeed. Since when?[7]

ﻬ ﻬ ﻬ

Tanya Meyers wanted to do something about the growing illiteracy crisis in her community. Adults who can't read face the problems of recurring unemployment, limited opportunity, and incessant embarrassment every day of their lives. Tanya knows that only too well—from her own first hand experience. Even though she graduated from public high school with passable grades she, like millions of other young Americans, never really learned to read.

"At first, I was able to fake it," she said. "I got a good job. I memorized what I needed to know. And I just sloughed through the rest. But that can be a miserable experience after awhile."

So, Tanya decided to teach herself how to read. "It wasn't easy, I'll tell you that. But I was determined. I worked real hard. After about two years, I felt confident enough to try to take some night classes at the local community college."

Tanya went on to get her degree in education. She got a new job as a teacher in an inner-city elementary school. "I decided that I would try to make a difference in kids lives long before they would have to face all the heartache that I had to face. I soon discovered that the parents were just as needy as the students. So, I decided to try to find a way to help them too."

Tanya found out about an innovative federally funded literacy program for adults. She went through the certification process, plowed through all the paperwork, obtained the funding, solicited and trained several volunteers, and solidified community support. All she needed was a suitable location. First she tried the schools. No luck, they were all overused already. The community's other public facilities were equally booked up. Then she checked into lease space. Too expensive. Soon she had run out of alternatives. When she happened to mention her dilemma to her pastor after church one Sunday, he immediately offered the congregation's ample facilities at no charge.

Tanya was thrilled. She scheduled classes, began signing up pupils, and distributed hundreds of fliers.

That was when the trouble began. Late one afternoon, Tanya received a call from a law office threatening an injunction that would effectively shut down the program. The attorney said that the program was an "unconstitutional establishment of religion and violation of the principle of the separation of church and state."

"I tried to explain the situation to him. I told him that the church really had nothing to do with the program — they were just providing the facilities. But he just held his ground."

Ultimately, the injunction was obtained, classes were canceled, and Tanya lost her funding. And the illiteracy rate continues unabated.[8]

ta ta ta

Marta Elliot thought she could short-circuit her problems. Instead she only compounded them.

"When I found out at the school clinic that I was pregnant, I was absolutely terrified," she said. "But, the nurse told me not to worry. She said that she could take care of everything—and that my parents wouldn't even have to find out about it. It all sounded so easy. I just let her make all the arrangements."

Because a "parental consent law" had recently gone into effect in her state, those "arrangements" involved not only an appointment at a local Planned Parenthood abortion chamber, but a consultation with a lawyer as well.

The nurse, the counselor at Planned Parenthood, and the lawyer all told Marta the same thing: she had a "good case" and thus, she would have no problem "getting around" the parental consent requirement. Barring any "unexpected complications," everything could be worked out in a single afternoon.[9]

The nurse didn't run into any unexpected complications in getting Marta excused from school the next day. The counselor at Planned Parenthood didn't run into any unexpected complications in securing Title XX funding for Marta's "surgical procedure." The lawyer didn't run into any unexpected complications in getting a judge to waive the "legal obstacles" posed by Marta's "minor status." In fact, everything ran like clockwork.

Everything that is, until Marta began hemorrhaging profusely from a lacerated cervix—an all too frequent "unexpected complication" of "safe and legal" abortion.[10] "During the ambulance ride to the hospital I was so lonely and afraid.

All I could think about was how much I wished my mother was there, about how wrong I had been about this whole thing, and about how manipulated I felt."

By the time she arrived at the emergency room, Marta was hanging on for dear life. But she still had the presence of mind to ask a doctor to notify her mother — something, by all "rights," she should have done in the beginning.[11]

≈ ≈ ≈

All the kids were excited. And well they should have been. They had worked hard on their parts for weeks on end. Their teacher, Lissa Coniaris, had really put them through the paces — as she had kids in that elementary school for the past eighteen years.

It was all about to pay off though. Dress rehearsal for the Christmas pageant was about to begin. The costumes were all aflutter. The smell of greasepaint filled the air. Proud parents snapped photos and circled the cacophonous scene with video cameras whirring.

But then came the bad news. The school's principal made his way across the auditorium, through the crowd, and up to Mrs. Coniaris. He pulled her aside and told her that the program had to be called off. Not postponed. Not rescheduled. But canceled altogether. The principal was chagrined. Mrs. Coniaris was flabbergasted. The parents were outraged. And the children were crushed. But there was absolutely nothing that any of them could do about it.

It seems that a member of the district's school board had been notified by a local attorney that the Christmas pageant constituted a "gross violation" of "the endorsement and establishment clauses of the First Amendment." He warned that, should the program be presented, the district would be placed in a very precarious legal position.

And what was it that made the pageant this year such legal contraband? "Well," Mrs. Coniaris explained, "toward the end of the program the kids were to sing a medley of carols—'Silent Night' and 'Away in a Manger' and a couple of others. Really, it wasn't going to be any different than what we'd done every year for the last eighteen years. But, I guess even that kind of moderate expression of our culture's Judeo-Christian roots is now illegal. It's like stories we used to hear about coming out of Russia. I just can't believe that something like this can happen here in America."

But it does. It happens here in America all the time.[12]

෨ ෨ ෨

Bill Hargess is the pastor of a small, but growing, suburban church. Concerned that his congregation faithfully communicate the Gospel in both word and deed he has, in the last couple of years, initiated a number of innovative ministries and outreaches—to the poor, to the homeless, to single adults, to latch-key kids, and to illegal aliens. He has also led the church into active involvement in the anti-pornography and pro-life movements as well.

"I have seen tremendous growth in the lives of our families," he said. "And, I have to attribute it to the fact that we are now, perhaps for the first time, seeing how the Lordship of Christ and the Bible really apply to the everyday dilemmas and details of life."

Now, Pastor Hargess and his congregation have several new dilemmas and details to which they must apply the Lordship of Christ and the Bible. No longer do they have to merely content themselves with the challenges of finding proper medical care for indigent families, or of setting up pre-natal care and counseling for pregnant teens, or of securing a mechanic to work on the car of a single mother, or of any number of the other "mundane" tasks that they tackle every week.

Now, they must fight for their very existence.

Several months ago, Pastor Hargess was notified by the Internal Revenue Service that the church's non-profit, tax-exempt status had been challenged by several "community citizens' groups" who had become concerned that the church's "non-religious, politically-motivated activities" violated the "spirit and intent of the law." Particularly of concern to the IRS was the church's pro-life picketing and rescuing. As a consequence of this concern, the church's bulk mailing permit was revoked, its bank account frozen, and its membership—and "all those working in concert with" its membership—were enjoined from further protests until a full investigation could be launched and a hearing scheduled.

"Even if we did not have solid Scriptural warrant," Pastor Hargess said, "or twenty centuries of church history as a precedent for the kinds of mercy ministries that we've been involved in, this kind of blatant persecution and suppression simply cannot be tolerated—at least not here in America where basic civil and human rights are supposed to be protected. I asked the IRS if it was now against the law to practice the Golden Rule. They didn't answer me directly, but they did promise me that they would conduct a thorough investigation."

These days, such investigations leave no good stone unturned. But then, they leave no good turn unstoned either.[13]

                                   ૐ ૐ ૐ

When Layle French bought a new home for his family, he decided to rent their former home until the real estate market improved enough that he could sell it. He thought it might even be a good investment for the future and an added source of new income for the family.

He was wrong.

Not long afterwards, he was notified that he was being sued for discriminatory business practices and a violation of the Minnesota Civil Rights Act. And as a result, he and his young family are facing utter financial ruin.

What was the heinous crime that he committed? What evil did he perpetrate to bring down this disaster? Very simply, he refused to rent his house to an unmarried couple because of his Christian concerns and convictions about premarital sex.

The Attorney General's office had received complaints from an attorney representing a woman and her live-in lover, that French had "illegally attempted to enforce his religious prejudices concerning marital status on the marketplace," and was thus "guilty of violating the couple's civil rights."

"They're pretty consistent in telling us that we can't push our religion on somebody else," Layle said. But, in fact, "they are trying to push their beliefs on us."

As if that were something new.[14]

                     ⱥ ⱥ ⱥ

Barry and Marsha Leddler have been quietly demonstrating their commitment to the sanctity of human life for the past eight years in a number of different ways. Marsha serves as a volunteer counselor at a crisis pregnancy center for teens near a local high school. Barry leads a community coalition of men who provide pro-life news and information to local legislators, hospital administrators, and business leaders. And together, each Saturday morning, they do sidewalk counseling outside a particularly notorious Planned Parenthood abortion chamber.

Recently, they decided to participate in a larger protest organized by a local Operation Rescue group. They had no idea how momentous that decision would be.

"The way the media talked about it later, you would have thought that some Libyan terrorists had sealed off half of

Pittsburgh," Marsha said. "Actually, it was like a really beautiful prayer meeting—with Bible reading, hymn singing, and quiet devoted prayer. No shouting. No shoving. There is no way that anyone could call what we did out there *violent harassment* or anything even *close* to that."

Apparently, the police thought differently. And so did the lawyers who were advising them. With brutal efficiency, they arrested more than one hundred of the peaceful men and women praying on the sidewalk and in the parking lot—including Barry and Marsha. "The men were transported to the North Side Police station where we were forced to go without food for over thirty-three hours," Barry said. "A couple of diabetic and hypoglycemic men had to be rushed to a hospital emergency room for treatment of food deprivation."

"The women went to the North Side station at first, but were then moved to the Allegheny County jail," Marsha said. "It was awful. The prison guards were unbelievably rough. Several of us were grabbed by the fronts of our blouses and bras. Some even had their breasts totally exposed and fondled in full view of the other prisoners."

The next day, a number of the protesters were moved again, at the behest of the attorneys advising city and county officials—this time to the Mayview Psychiatric Hospital. "I couldn't believe it," Barry related. "They actually held us in the psych ward for nearly two days. I thought things like that could only happen behind the Iron Curtain."

Well, that was then. And, this is now.[15]

         ತಿ ತಿ ತಿ

As diverse as they may appear to be at first glance, each of these frighteningly real legal scenarios have any number of very crucial elements in common:

Each one actually occurred during the past eighteen months.

Each one involved ordinary people — just like you or me — not powerful political lobbies, affluent commercial interests, or resourceful social movements. Just ordinary people.

Each one cost those ordinary people a lot of time, money, and heartache.[16]

Each one represents a gross miscarriage of justice and a violation of basic Constitutional and human rights.

And, each one was provoked, perpetrated, pursued, and plainted by attorneys affiliated with the American Civil Liberties Union.[17]

2

A VERY RESPECTABLE HERESY

suadet lingua, jubet vita[1]

If you ask me why I put Latin in my writing, it is because I have to show that it is connected with the Universal Fountain and with the European Culture, and with all that heresy combats.[2]

Hilaire Belloc

The word "heresy" not only means no longer being wrong; it practically means being clear-headed and courageous. The word "orthodoxy" not only no longer means being right; it practically means being wrong.[3]

G.K. Chesterton

During the 1988 presidential campaign, several public opinion polls revealed that the American Civil Liberties Union had a negative rating with the American people ranging anywhere from fifty-six to eighty-three percent.[4] Even by its own accounting,the ACLU is "the most hated organization in America."[5]

It has been openly criticized and castigated by the Attorney General of the United States.[6] It has been dubbed a "national criminals' lobby" by other high-level federal officials.[7] It has been dragged in front of the Congressional Committee for Un-American Activities to defend its tumultuous record.[8] It has been tarred and feathered as a "Communist-Front Organization" by groups as divergent as the American Legion[9] and the Legal Affairs Council,[10] the American Family Association[11] and the Patrick Henry League,[12] the Freedom Council[13] and the Church League of America,[14] the National Advisory Council[15] and the John Birch Society.[16] It has been pummeled in electoral campaigns.[17] It has been made the brunt of snide jokes and leering denigrations.[18] It has been targeted by pro-family and pro-life groups for its amoral policy positions.[19] It has been crudely caricatured by partisans of the Right for being too radical.[20] It has been rabidly ridiculed by partisans of the Left for not being radical enough.[21] And though "heresy" is not a word that has much currency in this day of overweening forbearance, it has even been dubbed "heretical."[22]

But, if it is a "heresy," it is "a very respectable heresy."[23] The fact is, despite all the animosity aimed its way — or perhaps, because of it — the ACLU has done quite well for itself.

The organization has never been, for instance, without its defiant defenders:

- General Douglas MacArthur: "The ACLU's crusade for civil liberties has had a profound and beneficial influence upon the course of American progress."[24]

- Governor Thomas Dewey: "Without the American Civil Liberties Union there would be no organization to take up the cudgels for lone, oppressed individuals."[25]

- President Harry Truman: "The integrity of the American Civil Liberties Union and of its workers in the field have performed outstanding service to the cause of true freedom."[26]

- President Dwight Eisenhower: "The members of the American Civil Liberties Union, with the overwhelming majority of my fellow citizens, are working together to combat every threat to our sacred principles of freedom, liberty, and equal justice under law with steadfast vigor and understanding."[27]

- President Lyndon Johnson: "Its unremitting fight against injustice and intolerance in this country and across the world has earned the ACLU the warm gratitude of countless individuals."[28]

- Supreme Court Chief Justice Earl Warren: "It is difficult to appreciate how far our freedoms might have eroded had it not been for the ACLU's valiant representation in the courts of the constitutional rights of the people of all persuasions."[29]

- American Bar Association: "We must remember that a right lost to one is lost to all. The ACLU remembers and it acts. The cause it serves so well is an imperative of freedom."[30]

- *The New York Times*: "The American Civil Liberties Union is a useful and thoroughly patriotic organization."[31]

- *The New Orleans Item*: "The ACLU is a controversial organization, yes, one that has had the courage to take an unpopular stand more than once. It has defended the constitutional rights of citizens of various creeds and political beliefs because it believes that if any American is deprived of his liberties, all of us are in danger. So, on its record, the ACLU would seem to be about as subversive as the Bill of Rights."[32]

- *The St. Louis Post-Dispatch*: "The ACLU has established its fiercely independent reputation by years of even-handed defense of principle — the freedom principle of the Bill of Rights."[33]

- *The Pittsburgh Post-Gazette*: "What the ACLU really stands for is the essence of Americanism."[34]

All that amounts to rather high praise. And it is not just boosters of the ACLU that have offered the organization such laudatory commendations. Over the years, even its severest critics have had to grudgingly admit that indeed, it has earned "respectability" for its "heresy":

- William F. Buckley, Jr.: "The ACLU is the most prestigious organization of its kind in the world."[35]

- William A. Donohue: "Although there are many other organizations that contribute to the making of American democracy, in the field of civil liberties the ACLU has no rival."[36]

- Nat Hentoff: "The ACLU is the only large-scale national organization whose primary client is the Bill of Rights and the Fourteenth Amendment."[37]

- Richard and Susan Vigilante: "For over sixty years the American Civil Liberties Union has been the nation's most able and dedicated advocate of the liberties guaranteed us in the Bill of Rights. It has defended free speech and opposed censorship; it has fought for racial equality; and, in labor disputes it has defended the rights of workers and bosses alike."[38]

- *Insight Magazine*: "The American Civil Liberties Union has always been at the center of a fire storm of controversy. What started as a champion of free speech rights

for radicals and protesters has become the most prestigious civil rights organization in the United States."[39]

The most common complaint of the critics of the organization is that, "Even though it is terribly liberal on many issues, and entirely out-to-lunch on most others, it does seem
to do a lot of good things here and there."[40] One critic, often
noted for his vitriolic attacks on the ACLU even went so far
as to admit that, "If the organization didn't exist, we would
have to invent something like it."[41]

What kind of organization is the ACLU, that it has been
able to evoke such paradoxical responses to its work — extreme opposition and vitriolic criticism on the one hand, and
admitted prestige on the other? How has it managed to so
polarize public opinion and still somehow maintain a position
in this country's judicial mainstream? If the ACLU is indeed
"heretical," how has it been able to drape the cloak of "respectability" over itself?

Organizational Vigilance

The ACLU is the world's oldest, largest, and most influential association of lawyers, political activists, and social reformers.[42] For more than seventy years[43] it has claimed a sin-
gle-minded devotion to protecting the Constitutional rights of
every citizen in the United States through lobbying, legislation, and most especially, litigation.[44]

Along the way, the organization has achieved a number
of remarkable successes — more often than not, dramatically
transforming the nature of America's legal and judicial system. With only 250,000 contributing members,[45] seventy staff
lawyers,[46] and a budget of approximately fourteen million dollars,[47] it has established more standing court precedents than
any other entity outside the Justice Department,[48] and it has
appeared before the Supreme Court more often than anybody

else except the government itself.[49] Some of its landmark cases include:

- 1920—The Palmer Raids Case: The ACLU combated Attorney General Mitchell Palmer over the deportation of a number of resident aliens who had been convicted of violent labor disruptions or who had been proven to be actively involved in various communist subversive activities throughout the country.

- 1921—The Draft Amnesty Campaign: The ACLU launched a nationwide drive to release draft objectors and convicted subversives following the First World War.

- 1924—The Patterson Strike Case: The ACLU defended a group of textile union members and other social activists (including the ACLU's own founder, Roger Baldwin) who launched a large-scale strike and illegally occupied private property.

- 1925—The Scopes Monkey Trial: The ACLU launched its "manipulated test case" strategy against the state of Tennessee's education standards, locating a small town biology teacher to act as a plaintiff and a showcase lawyer to focus national attention on the issue. Despite the fact that the ACLU and its high profile defender, Clarence Darrow, lost to the state's attorney William Jennings Bryan, the publicity proved to be invaluable.

- 1927—The Sacco and Vanzetti Case: The ACLU served the defense of two notorious anarchists who had been convicted of murdering two men during a payroll robbery. With a long list of ties to the subversive socialist underground, Sacco and Vanzetti sealed the ACLU's reputation as a radical instrument of the Left for some time to come.

- 1929 — The Gastonia Case: The ACLU defended seven striking workers who had been convicted of murdering a North Carolina police chief during a particularly violent confrontation. After declaring their anti-Christian and communist beliefs, the seven defendants jumped bail and fled to the Soviet Union.

- 1931 — The Scottsboro Case: The ACLU and the communist-led International Labor Defense worked together to overturn the convictions of nine black men who had been found guilty of raping two white women on a freight train. Sentences for all nine were reduced or reversed.

- 1933 — The *Ulysses* Case: The ACLU led the anti-censorship battle over a novel by English author James Joyce, which had been banned because of U.S. obscenity laws.

- 1942 — Japanese Internment Case: The ACLU failed to respond at first, but later was persuaded to take up the cause of Japanese-Americans who had been improperly detained in isolation camps just after the Pearl Harbor attack launched U.S. involvement in the Second World War.

- 1943 — Jehovah's Witnesses' Suit: The ACLU secured the right of children in the public schools to refuse to salute the flag or to recite the Pledge of Allegiance on religious grounds.

- 1950 — Loyalty Oaths Campaign: The ACLU fought McCarthy era requirements that public officials forswear any involvement with communist or subversive organizations.

- 1952 — Hollywood Blacklisting Campaign: The ACLU led the crusade against what it called "Red Baiting" in the entertainment industry.

- 1954 — Brown v. The Board of Education: Although not directly involved in the development of this crucial and historic school desegregation case, the ACLU filed an amicus brief in support of the NAACP's arguments before the Supreme Court.

- 1957 — Smith Act Reversal: The ACLU supported the defense of fourteen men convicted of conspiracy to violently overthrow the government of the United States. Lawyers argued on First Amendment free speech grounds.

- 1960 — Nativity Scenes Ban: The ACLU launched several legal initiatives to prohibit Christmas decorations or the singing of carols in public schools or on public property.

- 1962 — Regent's Prayer Case: In this case — one of several anti-prayer suits that the ACLU was involved in — lawyers argued that a prayer recited each day in the New York public schools, constituted an unlawful "establishment of religion."

- 1963 — The Gideon Case: In an important precedent, the ACLU won the right of every defendant to be provided a state appointed attorney.

- 1969 — The Tinker Case: The ACLU won the right of public school students to protest against the Viet Nam War by wearing black arm bands.

- 1973 — Doe v. Bolton: In this "manipulated test case," the ACLU led the legal fight that, in conjunction with the infamous Roe v. Wade ruling, eventually overturned the restrictive abortion laws in all fifty states.

- 1974 — Nixon Impeachment: The ACLU abandoned its facade of political neutrality by pursuing, in both the media and through legal channels, the impeachment of President Richard Nixon.

- 1976 — Christmas Pageants Ban: The ACLU has long fought against any form of public demonstration of religious faith. In this case they brought suit in New Jersey in an effort to prohibit Christmas pageants in the public schools.

- 1977 — The Skokie March: The ACLU shocked its liberal support by defending the right of American Nazis to march through a predominantly Jewish suburb of Chicago.

- 1981 — Newark School Board Case: The ACLU took this case in an attempt to prohibit the Gideons from distributing Bibles to students in the public schools on the grounds that such programs constitute a violation of the "separation of church and state."

- 1982 — Arkansas Creationism Case: Fifty-six years after it had argued against educational exclusionism in the Scopes Trial, the ACLU reversed itself, fighting against the right to teach various views of origins in public school classrooms.

- 1983 — The Akron Case: The ACLU successfully fought to overturn the right of localities to regulate the medical safety and the proper disclosure of abortion-related businesses.

- 1986 — Jager v. Douglas County: The ACLU was able to forbid religious invocations before high school football games. For the first time, the lawyers successfully used "endorsement" language instead of the traditional "establishment" language — the implication being that the government is not only forbidden to establish or institutionalize religion, it is forbidden to endorse or condone it as well.

- 1987—The Bork Confirmation: Once again abandoning all pretense of political neutrality, the ACLU led the smear campaign designed to deny Judge Robert Bork confirmation to the Supreme Court.

- 1988—Civil Rights Restoration Act: The Washington office of the ACLU led the four-year-long legislative battle to overturn the Supreme Court's Grove City decision, thus requiring institutions receiving federal grants to extend privileged service access to homosexuals, abortionists, and drug abusers.

- 1989—Equal Access Act: The ACLU was successful in making voluntary student prayer or Bible study meetings before or after school the one exception to the federal Equal Access Act of 1984. So, while students may gather in public schools to discuss Marxism, view Planned Parenthood films, play Dungeons and Dragons, listen to heavy metal rock, or hold gay activist club gatherings, they are not allowed to pray or read the Bible together.

By any standard this long list of achievements is remarkable. And, considering the fact that the ACLU no longer has to take many of its cases before the bench — its influence is so great that even a *threat* of a lawsuit is often enough to change policies, reshape legislation, and redirect priorities in case after case[50] — those achievements are even more remarkable.

And if that weren't enough, considering the very obvious anti-Christian and Leftist slant that most of the ACLU's landmark cases take — the almost omnipresent and omnipotent impression that the ACLU has obviously had in our courts and in our culture, transforming liberty into license — those remarkable achievements take on even greater significance. Most Americans adamantly abhor the causes the ACLU defends. Most public officials are ideologically opposed to the policy programs that the ACLU proposes. And most judges dread the sight of an ACLU brief. Yet, the successes of the organization continue to stack up. Its influence continues to grow. It may be a "heresy,"[51] but it is a "very respectable heresy." Very respectable indeed.

Early on, the ACLU took as its motto and rallying cry the apothegm of the nineteenth century radical abolitionist Wendell Phillips: "Eternal vigilance is the price of liberty."[52] Interestingly, it is its "organizational vigilance" that provides the key to understanding its "eternal vigilance." The ACLU is a model of efficiency. That fact alone is enough to explain its remarkable successes through the years.

The ACLU is actually a carefully decentralized grassroots network of fifty-one separately incorporated affiliates, over four hundred local chapters, and approximately five thousand volunteer lawyers from coast to coast.[53] Each of the local groups has a great deal of autonomy, operating its financial and legal affairs with virtually no interference or intrusion from the national office. Even the policies set forth in ACLU publications are not determined at the national level by the board of directors, but through a complex weighted-delegate and referendum system among the local groups.[54] The national office provides a number of crucial support services — coordinating national efforts, providing technical research, managing publicity and fund raising programs, spearheading publishing efforts, focusing affiliate vision, maintaining a legislative and lobbying presence, developing long range goals, launching special educational projects, and pooling resources for federal appellate cases — but by and large, each of the local chapters and affiliates are free to choose which civil liberties issues it will stress, which cases it will take to court, which political campaigns it will actively participate in, and which local legislation it will either support or oppose.[55] Each elects its own governing boards, hires its own staff, and develops its own budget.[56] Thus, even though all of the affiliates share common goals, common policy directives, and common resources, they are driven by the engines of local concern and the exigencies of local issues.[57]

Ultimately, it is this decentralization of its organization that has made the ACLU so devastatingly effective. It is diverse and yet cohesive. It is flexible and yet focused. It is circumscribed and yet broad based. Bureaucracy is virtually eliminated. Costs are held to a bare minimum. And, efficiency is tuned to a fever pitch.

The brash young nineteenth century Englishman of letters, Percy Bysshe Shelley, boasted that, "Poets are the unacknowledged legislators of the world."[58] Just based on the experience of the ACLU, a case could probably be made for the alternative proposition that, "Grassroots organizers are the unacknowledged legislators of the world." Conservative coalitions, legal associations, constitutional federations, pro-family organizations, church denominations, and even governmental institutions have been unable to stymie the grassroots effectiveness of the ACLU. They have in fact, all been steamrolled by its unrelenting efficiency.

Unfettered by the typical institutional restraints of top-down administration, the ACLU has been able to strategically mobilize its vastly outnumbered forces, and thus to win hopelessly unpopular causes. By remaining small, agile, and tractable, it has been able to carefully pick its cases, jurisdictions, courts, judges, and appellate paths. Instead of passively following the ponderous course of the judicial process, it harnesses the intricacies and oddities of that process to its own advantage. Localization allows the ACLU to discover those intricacies and oddities. National affiliation allows it to exploit them.

The bottom line is that the ACLU has done its homework *on* every single community and every single court in the country—because it does its homework *in* every single community and every single court in the country. It has been able to be "Johnny on the spot," actively litigating approximately six thousand cases at any given time.[59]

Form Follows Function

This decentralized system is not simply a management *technique*. It is integral to what the ACLU is, not just how it operates. To use the terminology of contemporary architectural design: in the inner-workings of the ACLU, form follows function. Its organizational vigilance is integral to its essence. According to Garland Swinney, a legal strategist for the conservative National Advisory Council think-tank:

> A major part of the ACLU's success can only be attributed to its innate and natural organizational structure. It certainly isn't the popularity of its positions. It is simply its brilliantly designed organic structure: it is not an institution; it is a *movement*. When you get right down to it, that is the only way to describe the ACLU: a grassroots reform *movement*. People don't belong to it like they would some club or professional association. If they belong, they are *true believers*. They are participants in a *cause*. And that makes all the difference in the world.[60]

This insight into the dynamic that drives the ACLU was confirmed by Roger Baldwin, the founder and creative force behind the organization all through the years until his death in 1981. He asserted:

> The ACLU is a private organization, and a private organization is like a church. You don't take non-believers into the church. We are a church; we have a creed and only true believers should lead us.[61]

The ACLU does not have a decentralized grassroots organizational structure because some slick management consultant convinced the leadership of its pragmatic virtues. It has that kind of structure because that is its *nature*. The ACLU is not simply a corporate entity. It is not simply a political action committee. And it is not simply a legal advocacy group. It is a *cause* that men rally to, sacrifice for, and find identity in. It is a *movement*. It is a *cabal*. It is a *faith*. Albeit, an "heretical" one.

This basic and fundamental fact is crucial to comprehend if any sense is to be made of the ACLU's glaring paradoxes and ribald ironies: the very thing that makes the ACLU so unpopular — its "heretical" faith — is also what makes it so successful and "respectable."

The Power of Faith

In Elijah's day, the prophets of Baal were men of influence, power, and position (see 1 Kings 16:29–34). They were well-respected members of the establishment (see 1 Kings 18:19). They were esteemed by the royalty and citizenry alike (see 1 Kings 18:20–21).

That had not always been the case though. In the past, Baalism had been widely understood to be a "heresy" — a twisting of the truth, a manipulation of life, liberty, and righteousness, and a rebellion against the Sovereign and Almighty God (see 1 Kings 15:9–14). In those days, it was not even a "respectable heresy." It was just "heresy."

But the prophets of Baal remained undeterred. They were *true believers*. For them, Baalism was not a fraternal order. It was not a voluntary association. It was not an advocacy group. It was a *cause* for them to rally to, sacrifice for, and find identity in. It was a *movement*. It was a *cabal*. It was a *faith*. And so, they went to work. They organized. They propagandized. They launched grassroots mobilization and infiltration strategies. They were less interested in popularity contests than they were in political conquests.[62]

Of course, the prophets of Baal had a real uphill battle on their hands. After all, the people of Israel had tasted the goodness of the Lord. They had witnessed first-hand His great and mighty deeds. And they had seen the impotence of the Caananite Pantheon before Him. But, strict adherence to a faith — even to a false and impotent faith — becomes a "fire in the minds of men."[63] True believers are driven. They are passionate. They are revolutionary. They are unconcerned with mere "facts." In fact, as historian Paul Johnson has said:

> Anxious as they are to promote their redeeming, transcending *truth*, the establishment of which they see as their mission on behalf of humanity, they have not much patience with the mundane, everyday truths represented by objective facts which get in the way of their arguments. These awkward minor truths get brushed aside, doctored, reversed, or are even deliberately suppressed.[64]

And so, the prophets of Baal pressed on against all odds, making their case and promoting their cause whenever and wherever they possibly could.

As a result of all their frantic and frenetic activity, the prophets of Baal ultimately won. At first, they only won "respectability" for their heresy. But then later, they won over the entire society. They established the cultural consensus.

In the face of that consensus, it would take great courage to face down the prophets and the newly installed Baalistic system. It would take great faith (see 1 Kings 18:25–36). Thankfully, Elijah was a man who had both. Once he began to exercise that courage and faith, the house of cards that the prophets of Baal had built with their passionate devotion, suddenly collapsed around them — as "heresies" always do (see 1 Kings 18:37–45).

As powerful a force as "heretical" faith may be, it is simply no match for faith in the genuine article — if and when faith in the genuine article is advanced at all.

That is the catch though, isn't it?

Conclusion

The ACLU seems to be a complex contradiction. It is hated. But it is grudgingly admired as well. It is widely regarded as an organization that contradicts in word and deed all that we hold dear in American society: freedom, morality, responsibility, and justice — in a word, it is a "heresy." And yet, it is a heresy that is held in high regard because of its undeniably successful track record in the courts.

The decentralized grassroots structure of the organization is surely a major ingredient in the ACLU's recipe for success. Because of that structure, it is able to maintain a significant, almost dominating, presence in virtually every community throughout the country. It is able to remain flexible. It is able to respond to local situations and circumstances. And it is not encumbered by a lumbering beauracracy.

But, that structure was not adopted by the ACLU just because it works so well. That structure is part and parcel with what the organization innately is. It is a *cause,* a *movement,* and a *faith.* Its successes cannot be explained by the mere implementation of mechanical models of management techniques. Analyses of demographic trends, ideological shifts, statistical variations, and policy developments simply are inadequate measures of the ACLU. Clearly, it does what it does because it is what it is.

And the only way that the "heretical" agenda of the ACLU can be halted in its tracks is for us to respond in kind — doing what we do because we are what we are.[65]

PART TWO

THE FACTS

Spiritual conflict is more fruitful of instability in the state than conflict of any other kind.[1]

Hilaire Belloc

If you argue with a madman, it is extremely probable that you will get the worst of it; for in many ways his mind moves all the quicker for not being delayed by the things that go with good judgment. He is not hampered by a sense of humor, or by charity, or by the dumb certainties of experience.[2]

G.K.Chesterton

3

LAW, LIBERTY, AND LICENSE

mendacia nihil caro[3]

There is a moral strain, arising from the divergence between what our laws and moral phrases pretend, and what our society actually is.[4]

Hilaire Belloc

He who wills to reject nothing, wills the destruction of will; for will is not only the choice of something, but the rejection of almost everything.[5]

G.K. Chesterton

The American Civil Liberties Union does not advertise itself as a *cause*. Nor does it advertise itself as a *movement* or a *faith*. Instead, it advertises itself as an advocate of "truth, justice, and the American way." It advertises itself as the "lone defender" against prejudice, tyranny, and brutality.

Philosopher George Santayana has said that, "Advertising is the modern substitute for argument; its function is to make the worse appear the better."[6] Certainly, that appears to be the case with the ACLU. What it advertises itself as, and what it actually is, are two entirely different things.

"Modern men and movements," Jean Paul Sartre often argued, "ought not be adjudged by what they say, but rather by what they do."[7] Similarly, Friedreich Nietzsche asserted that, "If you wish to understand men and movements, do not merely ask what they say, but find out what they want."[8] Although neither Sartre nor Nietzsche had sound philosophies, in this case, their cautious discretion is a point well taken. The fact is, what the ACLU *wants* and ultimately *does* utterly belie what it *says*. That discrepancy then is the key to properly adjudging and understanding the organization.

Only One Client

The ACLU says that it "has only one client: the Bill of Rights."[9] It advertises itself as doggedly impartial, caring only about the integrity of the Constitution itself.[10]

But, the facts say otherwise.

The radical labor and social dissent movements have always been the ACLU's primary clients — the Constitution notwithstanding. In its very first annual report, the ACLU described itself as, "a militant, central bureau in the labor movement for legal aid, defense strategy, information, and propaganda."[11] It went on to assert that along with the International Workers of the World and the Communist Party, it was the "center of resistance" for radical groups in America.[12] In its advertising flier it argued that "The union of organized labor, the farmers, and the radical and liberal movements, is the most effective means . . . whereby rights can be secured and maintained. It is that union of forces which the American Civil Liberties Union serves."[13] Thirteen years later, the organization reaffirmed its commitment to the radical cause stating that, "the struggle between capital and labor is the most vital application of the principle of civil liberty."[14]

In 1976, Aryeh Neier, then the Executive Director of the ACLU, broadened the client base of the organization saying that it was "the legal branch of the women's movement."[15] In fact, as the years went by, the ACLU would identify with virtually every subversive dissent movement that appeared on the national scene: Communists, Anarchists, Socialists, terrorists, homosexuals, lesbians, pornographers, Nazis, abortionists, and Atheists.[16]

Even a cursory glance at the caseload of the ACLU demonstrates that it is far more interested in pursuing its ideological agenda than it is in defending the Constitution.[17]

Non-Partisan

The ACLU says that it is "wholly non-partisan."[18] It advertises itself as an objective organization that is "neither liberal nor conservative, Republican nor Democrat."[19] Instead, it is "a public interest organization devoted exclusively to protecting the basic civil liberties of all Americans."[20]

But, the facts say otherwise.

Roger Baldwin, the founder and leading force in the ACLU until his death in 1981, asserted the partisan nature of his agenda saying:

> I am for Socialism, disarmament, and ultimately for abolishing the state itself as an instrument of violence and compulsion. I seek social ownership of property, the abolition of the propertied class, and sole control by those who produce wealth. *Communism is the goal.* It all sums up into one single purpose — the abolition of dog-eat-dog under which we live.[21]

This attitude has marked the ACLU, to one degree or another, throughout its long history, so that William Donohue could accurately argue that:

Social reform, in a liberal direction, is the *sine qua non* of
the ACLU. Its record, far from showing a *momentary waver-
ing* from impartiality, is replete with attempts to reform
American society according to the wisdom of liberalism.
The truth of the matter is that the ACLU has always been
a highly politicized organization.[22]

In recent years, the ACLU has revealed its blatant parti-
sanship time after time. It vehemently opposed the Viet Nam
War.[23] It demanded unilateral nuclear disarmament.[24] It
called for disinvestment in South Africa.[25] It violated its own
policy in order to stymie the nomination of William Rehnqu-
ist to the Supreme Court.[26] It steadfastly opposed the Nixon
Administration and was the first organization to call for his
impeachment following Watergate.[27] During the eight years of
the Reagan Administration, it blasted the President with one
invective after another.[28] It led the fight to defeat the confirmation of Robert Bork to the Supreme Court.[29] It frequently
writes speeches for candidates that it likes.[30] And it even issues scorecards on legislators evaluating their performance according to the ACLU's own ideological yardstick.[31]

As Donohue has said, "Quite simply, the ACLU has a
politics, and that politics is liberalism."[32]

Champion of the Bill of Rights

The ACLU says that at the time that it was set up, during the furor of the First World War, "freedom of speech
didn't exist."[33] It then goes on to messianically advertise itself
as the only "nationwide, non-partisan organization dedicated
to preserving and defending the Bill of Rights."[34]

But, the facts say otherwise.

John Haynes Holmes, one of the ACLU's original board
members, confessed that the organization was only "using the
civil liberties issue," and that its real interest was "the cause
of radicalism."[35] He went so far as to say that the ACLU was

"manipulating" cases "as a means toward certain ends; namely, the advancement of labor and the revolution."[36] Roger Baldwin himself said that, "Civil liberties, like democracy are useful only as tools for social change."[37]

Perhaps that explains the curious inconsistency of the organization in its "defense" of the Bill of Rights. For instance, the Second Amendment of the Bill of Rights says that, "The right of the people to keep and bear arms shall not be infringed." But according to the ACLU *Policy Guide*, "The possession of weapons by individuals is not constitutionally protected."[38] The Tenth Amendment of the Bill of Rights says that, "The powers not delegated to the United States by the Constitution, nor prohibited by it to the states, are reserved to the states respectively, or to the people." But in 1985, the ACLU castigated the President and the Attorney General for suggesting that Tenth Amendment provisions be enforceable by law.[39] Over the years, the ACLU has variously opposed the enforcement of clauses in the First Amendment[40] and the Fifth Amendment.[41] It has defended the free speech, transit, and assembly rights of nuclear protesters[42] but has denied those same rights to abortion protesters.[43] It has fought for the right to strike for unions[44] but it has fought against the right to work for individuals.[45]

This hypocritical double standard has been so embarrassingly blatant that it was even castigated by the liberal journalist Walter Lippman:

> The ACLU almost never goes into action when the liberties of anyone on the Right are attacked . . . It has missed one opportunity after another to prove that it really stands for the thing it professes to stand for, that it cares for civil liberty as such, as a good thing in itself and not merely because it is a convenience for Communists, Anarchists, Socialists, and labor organizers.[46]

Far from being a "champion" of the Bill of Rights, the ACLU has proven to be one of its most stalwart foes.

The Right to Privacy

The ACLU says that, "The Constitution as originally conceived was deeply flawed."[47] In fact, it was not until the organization came along that the American ideals of freedom and justice could be realized. "The ACLU," it brazenly asserts, "was the missing ingredient that made our constitutional system finally work."[48] And so, it shows no hesitation in advertising itself as "the ignition for the constitutional engine, the key that makes it run."[49]

Part of this sense of self-importance stems from the ACLU's discovery—and enforcement in the courts—of the "right to privacy."[50] Everything from wire tapping to finger printing, drug testing to lie detectors, and breathalyzers to airport security measures have been ardently opposed by the organization on the basis of this "right."[51] Similarly, everything from abortion to euthanasia, homosexuality to pornography, and drug use to prostitution have been adamantly defended.[52]

Apparently, this liberal notion of "privacy" does not extend to everyone. Take the case of Illinois Congressman Henry Hyde. A prominent foe of abortion in the House and the author of Federal legislation to limit the use of tax dollars for the killing of unborn children, Hyde rankled the ire of ACLU officials. So, they plotted a course of retaliation: they hired a private investigator to report on the Congressman's leisure-time activities, to monitor his mail, and to compile a three-hundred page dossier on his private life.[53]

The ACLU has found exceptions to the "right to privacy" for any number of its other adversaries as well: non-union workers,[54] conservative judges,[55] police,[56] pro-lifers,[57] Christian evangelists,[58] parents of teens,[59] and concerned teachers.[60]

The notion of "privacy" that the ACLU is constantly bleating about is clearly less a "right" to be protected than a "weapon" to be wielded. As Mark Campisano, former Supreme Court clerk for Justice William Brennan, has asserted:

> An accounting of the ACLU's caseload suggests that the organization is an ideological chameleon—that beneath the protective coloration of *civil liberties*, the ACLU is pursuing a very different agenda, one contrary to basic principles of American constitutional democracy.[61]

Equal Protection

The ACLU says that the Constitution guarantees "the right to equal treatment regardless of race, sex, religion, national origin, sexual orientation, age, physical handicap, or other such classification."[62] Predictably, it advertises itself as a "constant and vigilant celebration" of that "basic constitutional principle."[63]

But, the facts say otherwise.

Time and again, the ACLU has opposed "equal protection" in favor of "preferential treatment."[64] It doesn't want homosexuals, lesbians, pornographers, and abortionists to receive equal treatment. It wants them to receive special privileges that other citizens do not enjoy.[65] That is why, through the years, it has supported every preferential entitlement program that has come down the pike: "compensatory justice,"[66] "remedial education,"[67] "ratios and quotas,"[68] "affirmative action,"[69] and "comparable worth."[70]

Not content with "equality of opportunity," the ACLU has pressed for "equality of outcome."[71] In its statement endorsing racial quotas it asserted that:

> The principle of non-discrimination requires that individuals should be treated individually in accordance with their personal merits, achievements, and potential, and not on the basis of the supposed attributes of any class or caste with which they may be identified.[72]

But then, it went on to take back all that fine "equal protection" rhetoric inconsistently saying that:

> When discrimination—and particularly discrimination in employment and education—has been long and widely practiced against a particular class, it cannot be satisfactorily eliminated merely by the prospective adoption of neutral, color-blind statements for selection among applicants for available jobs or educational programs.[73]

The result of this "discrimination to spite discrimination" approach to social and economic affairs has proven to be disastrous. Innumerable studies have shown that preferential entitlements actually debilitate and impoverish minorities—creating disincentives to advancement and engendering an artificial indolence.[74]

In any case, it is a far cry from the ACLU's purported allegiance to the principle of "equal protection." As Richard and Susan Vigilante have said, "There are few genuine civil liberties issues at stake today, and the devil makes work for idle hands."[75]

In the Mainstream

The ACLU claims that its positions are "mainstream positions."[76] Thus, it advertises itself as American as apple pie and baseball—or perhaps, even more American than that.[77]

But, the facts say otherwise.

The ACLU's position on almost any and every issue is diametrically opposed to "the mainstream" of American ethical and legal thought—as table 3.1, Official Policy Positions, clearly demonstrates:

Table 3.1 Official Policy Positions	
The ACLU Supports	*The ACLU Opposes*
Legalization of child pornography[78]	Voluntary school prayer[79]
Legalization of drugs[80]	Sobriety checkpoints[81]
Tax exemption for satanists[82]	Tax exemption for churches[83]
Legalization of prostitution[84]	Religious displays in public[85]
Abortion on demand[86]	Medical safety regulation and reporting[87]
Mandatory sex education[88]	Parental consent laws[89]
Busing[90]	Educational vouchers and home schooling[91]
Ideological testing for court appointees[92]	Governmental ethics committees[93]
Automatic entitled probation[94]	Prison terms for criminal offenses[95]
Public demonstrations for Nazis and communists[96]	Public demonstrations for direct action pro-lifers[97]
Legalization of polygamy[98]	Teaching "monogamous, heterosexual intercourse within marriage" in the public schools[99]

It is all too evident, as Mark Campisano has argued, the ACLU's policy positions have "a pernicious underlying theme: hostility to the processes of constitutional democracy." This appears, he says "in three basic forms: first, in attempts to override democratic processes and replace them with judicial decrees, in ever larger spheres of public life; second, in attempts to expand individual *rights* without regard for counter-vailing public interests; and third, in attempts to prevent certain viewpoints from being heard in the public arena."[100] Thus, far from being a part of America's mainstream, the ACLU is, according to constitutional lawyer Michael Palin, "completely out in *left* field."[101] Indeed as Reed Irvine has asserted, "ACLU is a four letter word meaning *liberal.*" [102]

Defend the SOBs

The ACLU says that, "Unless we defend the rights of the *sonsofbitches*, we'll lose our own."[103] Thus, it advertises itself as America's "watchdog for the underdog"—as the beach-head defense for citizens who face civil rights deprivation, regardless of who they are or what they believe.[104] "Sooner or later everybody needs the ACLU," says Executive Director, Ira Glasser. "When your constitutional rights are threatened, you'll come to the ACLU."[105] The implication is that the ACLU will then rush to your defense.

But, the facts say otherwise.

The ACLU only rushes to the aid of those that contribute to its *cause*, its *movement*, and its *faith*. The perception that it has a diverse portfolio of cases scattered all over the ideological map is, very simply, a myth. Although the organization has occasionally ventured out of the Left's territorial waters to defend such groups as the Ku Klux Klan,[106] the John Birch Society,[107] and even the Jews for Jesus,[108] without exception those cases have been carefully contrived either as public relations "showpieces" or as "back door precedents" for their own agenda.[109] In other words, they have been little more than a means to an end.

Roger Baldwin admitted as much when he wrote:

All my associates in the struggle for civil liberties take a class position, though many of them don't know it. I too take a class position. It is anti-capitalist and pro-revolutionary. I champion civil liberty as the best of the non-violent means of building the power on which the workers' rule must be based. If I aid the reactionaries to get free speech now and then, if I go outside the class struggle to fight against censorship, it is only because those liberties help to create a more hospitable atmosphere for working class liberties. The class struggle is the central conflict of the world; all others are incidental.[110]

So, the incidental case that the ACLU might deign to undertake for a non-radical, a conservative, a Christian, or an ordinary citizen — in Baldwin's parlance a "reactionary" — is little more than an "incidental" means to "create a more hospitable atmosphere" for its pet Leftist causes.

Conclusion

Things just aren't always as they seem. That is the dilemma of living in a fallen world. G.K. Chesterton brilliantly captured the essence of this dilemma when he wrote that:

The real trouble with this world of ours is not that it is an unreasonable world, nor even that it is a reasonable one. The commonest kind of trouble is that it is nearly reasonable, but not quite. Life is not an illogicality; yet it is a trap for logicians. It looks just a little more mathematical and regular than it is; its exactitude is obvious, but its inexactitude is hidden; its wildness lies in wait. . . . It is this silent swerving from accuracy by an inch that is the uncanny element in everything. It seems a sort of secret treason in the universe. An apple or an orange is round enough to get itself called round, and yet is not round after all. The earth itself is shaped like an orange in order to lure some simple astronomer into calling it a globe. A blade of grass is called after a blade of the sword, because it comes to a point; but it doesn't. Everywhere in things there is this element of the quiet and incalculable.[111]

Mirroring the world's falleness, the uncanny element in the ACLU is its silent swerving from accuracy by an inch. Its exactitude is obvious, but its inexactitude is hidden; its wildness lies in wait. It is almost operatic in its unreality — the perfect embodiment of that protean ostentation that has always marked the minions of student-cafe radicalism.

Things just aren't always as they seem.

4

A PURLOINED CONSCIENCE

hic jacet, umbra, cinis, nihil[1]

> *To comprehend the history of a thing is to unlock the mysteries of its present, and more, to disclose the profundities of its future.*[2]
>
> Hilaire Belloc

> *A liberal may be defined approximately as a man who, if he could, by waving his hand in a dark room, stop the mouths of all the deceivers of mankind forever, would not wave his hand.*[3]
>
> G.K. Chesterton

For at least the first hundred years of our nation's history, Boston was America's premier city. New York had emerged as the center for banking and commerce. Washington had outgrown its coarse backwater image to become cosmopolitan and powerful. Philadelphia continued in its role as the locus for publishing and industry. St. Louis and Chicago had come into their own as gateways into the land's vast interior. San Francisco was a vibrant mercantile hub on the edge of the world. And the great cities of the South — Richmond,

Charleston, and Atlanta—were genteel and refined showcases of America's rich agricultural ethos. But Boston set the pace. In a very real sense, she defined the soul of America.

Boston had been the cradle of the American Revolution—and the heartbeat of the Constitutional process. She gave the young nation some of the finest thinkers, most adamant reformers, and most dedicated patriots the world had ever seen—from John Adams to Ralph Waldo Emerson, from Phillips Brooks to Henry David Thoreau, from Paul Revere to Henry Cabot Lodge. She led in culture, education, religion, politics, and finance—the home of Harvard University, the Brattle Theatre, the New England Conservatory of Music, and the Boston Athenaeum. Every great movement that swept across the rapidly expanding Republic seemed to begin with her—from the Great Awakening to Transcendentalism, from Manifest Destiny to Abolitionism, from Reform Progressivism to Unitarianism.

As a result of this heady and free-wheeling culture, the privileged upper-crust citizens of Boston were a breed apart. They tended to be advanced in their thinking, progressive in their ideals, and dogmatic in their resolve. They were, more often than not, passionately unyielding in their utopian vision for reform. They were staunchly independent. They were liberal. They were quintessentially Yankee.

Into this meliorative milieu was born Roger Nash Baldwin on January 21, 1884. Both sides of his family could trace their ancestry back to the Pilgrim fathers and to what he would later refer to as "the inescapable *Mayflower.*"[4] Blue-blooded, prosperous, well educated, progressive, and civic minded, the Baldwin family ably transmitted to all their children the social and cultural aura of Boston. But it was perhaps most evident in this, their first-born. In fact, some ninety years later his biographer could say of him:

> Through all the eventful years of his life Roger Baldwin has remained exactly what he has always been—a proper Bos-

tonian. Put him, as indeed he has been put, behind bars in a New Jersey prison, in a Pennsylvania steel mill, in a dacha outside Moscow or an industrial farm in the Caucasus; put him in Geneva at the League of Nations, in New York at the United Nations; put him in London, Paris, Rome, Vienna; in Japan with General MacArthur, in St. Louis with Emma Goldman, in India with Jawaharlal Nehru; put him in mid-town Manhattan presiding over the affairs of the American Civil Liberties Union, or canoeing on the Ramapo River — still he emerges unmistakably and ever a Boston Brahmin. His craggy narrow face with its sharp patrician features, his piercing eyes, his slightly weatherbeaten look, his hurried purposeful gait are all pure Yankee.[5]

The inescapability of his Boston heritage colored all that he did throughout his life. And ultimately it colored all that the ACLU has done as well, because as Mrs. Evarts Graham asserted, "The American Civil Liberties Union is truly the length and shadow of Roger Baldwin."[6]

Certainly there were other strong influences on the character and development of the organization. Norman Thomas, who was six times the Socialist Party's candidate for President, was an original and very influential board member of the ACLU. Morris Hillquit, the outspoken and headstrong director of the National Executive Committee of the Socialist Party, was a key member of the ACLU's first National Committee. William Z. Foster, later the Chairman of the Communist Party U.S.A., was also a crucial founding member of the organization — as were Max Eastman, who served as the editor of the Communist Party's *The Masses*, Harry F. Ward, who, according to *The Congressional Record*,[7] maintained membership and affiliation with over two hundred Communist or Communist-Front organizations, and Clarence Darrow, who dazzled the nation as a flamboyant and articulate defense attorney and anti-Christian crusader. Undoubtedly, the ACLU was brought into existence by an impressive and volatile mix of scintillating minds and simmering passions. But Roger Baldwin was the dominant personality overshadowing all the others. The ACLU was by his own admission, "a one man show."[8] In fact, as the ACLU's first staff attorney, Arthur Garfield Hayes, often quipped, "the American Civil Liberties Union *is* Roger Baldwin."[9] Even now, nearly a decade after his death, Baldwin continues to be "the major personality in American civil liberties history," according to Alan Reitman, the Associate Director of the ACLU.[10]

"An organization is no more than the sum of its parts," argues author William McIlhany. "Its advocacies and actions are the ideas and work of its members, usually the more energetic and influential ones."[11] Clearly then, any examination of the ACLU must also, out of sheer necessity, include an examination of this remarkable man.

Origins of a Cause

Despite moderate wealth, prominence, and privilege, young Roger's home life was unstable and unhappy. It was in fact tragically marred by dissension, strife, adultery, and divorce. As a result, his strongest early influences were outside the home: his grandfather and aunt.

His grandfather, William Henry Baldwin, was an iconoclastic and nonconformist anti-Christian crusader whose controversial and dogmatic beliefs resulted in his expulsion from membership in the YMCA. He promptly helped to set up a rival organization and spent the rest of his life railing against any and all orthodoxies. Roger later would say that his grandfather was "the moving force" behind his "liberal" and "nonconformist" upbringing.[12]

His aunt, Ruth Standish Baldwin, was an avid social reformer and cocksure supporter of various utopian causes. She was a founder of the National Urban League, a trustee of Smith College, and a member of the Socialist Party. Of her, Roger said, "My almost saintly Aunt Ruth was an endless source of comfort and inspiration to me. She was wise, selfless, and sensitive. She shared my radicalism, but in her own more respectable way."[13]

Immersed in this world of radical reform early on, Roger developed a strong sense of what he called "the white man's burden."[14] He followed his grandfather into a life-long moralistic rebellion against the church. And he followed his aunt into a life-long association with anti-capitalist fringe groups.

It was "quite inevitable" that the youngster should formally cap his very traditional Boston education at Harvard. It was equally inevitable that his nascent radicalism should continue to develop in those environs. Harvard was, he said, "a place where dissent in any form was quite respectable."[15] It was in fact the very vortex of what was then called the Progressive Movement.

During the first decade of the twentieth century, urgent problems brought on by dramatic changes in the cultural and industrial landscape demanded immediate and innovative solutions. Progressivism offered such solutions. Under the dynamic leadership of President Theodore Roosevelt and his congressional proteges — Henry Cabot Lodge, Charles Lindbergh, Sr., and George Wharton Pepper — the movement produced a powerful groundswell of united support for sweeping social, political, and economic reforms. Rights were secured for organized labor; political machines were called into account; and massive commercial trusts were reined in.

Despite those remarkable successes, however, once Roosevelt left the White House, Progressivism splintered. Lodge, Lindbergh, and Pepper tried to carry on the President's tradition — informed by Christian conviction, patriotism, and family values. Among the movement's disparate factions and interests, there were however, a large number of irreverent and impatient young radicals who were informed by a very different ideological standard: the revolutionary philosophies and ideals of the European Enlightenment. They pushed the bulk of Progressivism into the fringes of American politics and cul-

ture, establishing dozens of groups intent on the utter decima-
tion of the national vision: the Mugwumps, the Anarchists,
the Knights of Labor, the Grangers, the Single Taxers, the
Suffragettes, the International Workers of the World, the
Populists, and the Communists.

Predictably, Roger and most of his friends at Harvard, in-
vested their impetuous ardor in one or another of these factions and sects. For many, such an investment was little more
than a youthful fascination. But for Roger it was the origin of
a *cause*.

Origins of a Faith

Following his graduation from Harvard, Roger spent a
gentlemanly year in touring Europe. But the life of the idle
rich — spending long aimless hours gazing out at the Mediter-
ranean from the marbled portico of an Italian palazzo or com-
pulsive shopping in the exclusive shops of Paris, London, and
Vienna — did not suit him well. Upon his return to Boston, he
at last began to seek out suitable employment.

Through his family connections, he was offered a job in
St. Louis managing a neighborhood settlement house and
teaching sociology at Washington University — despite never
even having taken a course in social ethics. Happily, he took
the job, leaving Boston and his life of leisure behind.

Immediately, he launched into a blinding flurry of activity. He became a faithful and devoted member of the Civic
League — an old line grassroots reform organization in the
city. He helped to organize the St. Louis City Club — a lun-
cheon group that was the focal point for political discus-
sions — and brought a number of prominent Suffragettes, Socialists, Anarchists, and Communists to town to speak. He
attended meetings of the IWW — the International Workers
of the World — a violent labor movement with a marked
Marxist flavor. He participated in local politics and helped
reformulate St. Louis municipal government. And of course,

he also busied himself with his classes at the University and with the youngsters at the settlement house.

It was still another of his activities though, that claimed a priority place in Roger's schedule. His work at the settlement house and in the surrounding neighborhood led him to invest more and more of his time in the juvenile court, and after a year, he was appointed chief probation officer. This was Roger's first introduction to the judicial system, and he quickly was consumed with its intricate details and seemingly unlimited possibilities. It soon became his chief passion.

At the time, the court was little more than a criminal bench. Not content with that, he marshalled his radical heritage and resources to pioneer the concept of *in loco parentis* — the court in the place of the parent — a concept that is still very much a part of our judicial system. Seeing his Progressive ideals implemented by the courts, revolutionized Roger's thinking. It was the beginning of a growing conviction that perhaps society could one day be fundamentally altered without violent insurrection, utilizing the courts to bypass conservative families, communities, and democratically elected institutions. He would recall later in life that it was then that he was "converted" to "judicial supremacy."[16] It was then that his *cause* was translated into a *faith*.

Origins of a Movement

During these busy and formative years, Roger fell under the sway of three strong-willed women — women that would wield great influence over him for the rest of his life: Anna Louise Strong, Margaret Sanger, and Emma Goldman.

Anna was his first true love — and his first betrothed. The daughter of a liberal minister from Seattle, she was beautiful, brilliant, and beguiling. She was a practicing journalist and a national leader in the newly emerging field of social work — and one of the few women with an earned Ph.D. in any discipline. Roger met her in 1910 when she came to St. Louis to arrange a child welfare exhibit. The two reformers quickly fell in love. After a brief courtship, they announced their engagement and Roger travelled with her back to the Northwest to meet her family.

The whirlwind romance ended suddenly however, when Roger refused to give up his smoking and drinking. Anna's puritanical liberalism — the ancient geomancy of a credo unique to the late nineteenth and early twentieth centuries — simply could not countenance that kind of indulgence. She was tearful but resolute.

While the love affair ended, the relationship did not — the two would stay in touch for the rest of their long lives. Anna went on to gain fame as an instigator of violent labor unrest and an advocate of Marxist insurgency. Following the Bolshevik Revolution, she renounced her American citizenship, moved to Moscow, and married a Soviet official. She continued to write and lecture widely with great effect internationally. During Stalin's purge, she was forced to flee her adopted homeland. She found refuge with Mao in Beijing where she lived out her days, ever the purist, ever the apologist, and ever the unwavering partisan.

Anna became for Roger an ideological conscience. She was his standard of commitment. She was as practical as potatoes and as pointed as a pikestaff. She demonstrated how to translate the lofty "ambition" of a *cause* and a *faith* into the hidden subtleties and harsh realities of life — into a real and tangible *movement*.

Margaret Sanger was, like Anna, a brilliant, beautiful, and beguiling woman of resolute action. When she met Roger in 1915, she was already a celebrated advocate of free love, eugenic birth limitation, and contraception.[17] During a nationwide speaking tour, she came to St. Louis only to be turned away from her rented hall by city officials and police concerned about her brazen public obscenity. Roger heard about the incident and rushed to her defense. He organized a public protest meeting outside the locked and barred auditorium.

Margaret and Roger became fast friends. And it was to be a lasting friendship. They continued to see each other socially for the next several decades.

Margaret's fame grew to almost mythic proportions as the renegade founder of Planned Parenthood. She almost single-handedly ushered in both the sexual and birth control revolutions. And she laid the framework for the modern recurrence of ethically justified abortion, euthanasia, infanticide, fetal experimentation, triage, surrogacy, and organ harvesting. But her triumphs did not come without great cost. She was arrested time and again. Once she was forced to sneak out of the country under the cover of night. She was reviled and rejected. Like Anna though, she was undeterred in her vision. She was as resolute as permafrost. She was as unflappable as a fat, bronzed Buddha.

Thus, Margaret became for Roger another paradigm of fidelity. Her example was impressive, vivid, and somehow terrible. In her, softer needs seemed to have remained stillborn. Everything in her life was subsumed in the *cause*. Even the breathy cabaret of her brazenness was submitted to the *faith*. She personified the *movement* like Chopin personified *pianissimo*. And she left her mark on Roger like Chopin left his on music.

Emma Goldman was brilliant, like Anna and Margaret. But unlike the other two, she was anything but beautiful and beguiling. Instead, she was baleful and brutal. Known as the "Red Queen of Anarchy," Emma was infamous as an advocate of violent revolution, political assassination, and Marxist Populism. Roger first saw her at one of her lectures — in a ramshackle smoke-filled hall in a disreputable St. Louis neighborhood. He was immediately wowed by her erudite discussion of philosophical profundities and ideological certainties. He initiated a correspondence with her that eventually blossomed into a deep and abiding friendship. Emma discipled the young reformer, introducing him to the literature of Ibsen, Tolstoy, and Kropotkin. She taught him the grassroots mobilization tactics of the great European revolutionary ca-

bals. She tutored his subversive impulse with the Enlightenment catechisms of Rousseau, Babeuf, Buonarroti, Nechayev,
and Lenin. She schooled him in the great verities of *humanism*: the self-sufficiency and inherent goodness of man, the
persistent hope of his perfectibility, and the relativity of all
ethical mores. She desensitized him to the most extreme ideas
and the most perverse confabulation ever devised by men.
She initiated him to their collusive mumblings as a druid
would beetle an acolyte into the darkness.

Later, Roger would say that Emma was, along with Anna
and Margaret, "one of the chief inspirations of his life."[18] Like
the other two, she had actually fleshed out the aspirations of
radical *humanism*. She had actually translated the *cause* and
the *faith* into a viable *movement*.

Civil Libertarian

Roger longed to emulate all three women. He feared the
hypocrisy of "Salon Socialism" and "Arm Chair Bolshevism" like
nothing else. Just when he began to fear that his nightmare ide-
alism would soon devolve into a more pragmatic disillusion-
ment, he got his chance to prove its mettle. That chance was an
invitation in 1917 to move to New York to work for the American Union Against Militarism — the AUAM.

The AUAM was a pacifist lobbying group organized by
Lillian Wald, Jane Addams, Paul Kellog and other prominent
liberals to counter the growing chorus of voices calling for
American involvement in the First World War. Their strategy
was calm and reasoned, based on their contacts and rapport
with the Wilson Administration in Washington. But, their effort proved to be too little too late.

Roger left St. Louis on April 2. On April 6, America officially joined the Allies in the "war to end all wars," in the
"war to make the world safe for democracy." By May 18, the
Selective Service Act had been railroaded through Congress
and signed into law.

Suddenly, the complexion of the AUAM's task had changed dramatically. At Roger's behest, and under his leadership, it turned its attention toward war resistance. Thus, the Bureau of Conscientious Objectors was founded on May 19, 1917. Set up in order to help draft dodgers develop practical strategies of resistance and to provide them with financial and legal support, the Bureau became the most active and the most visible branch of the AUAM.

Immediately, the Bureau caused a storm of controversy. *The New York Times* criticized it saying that Baldwin, and others working with him, were "antagonizing the settled policies of the government, resisting the execution of its deliberately formed plans, and gaining for themselves immunity from the application of laws to which all other good citizens willingly submit."[19]

In an attempt to quell the fears of the AUAM board and to duck some of the heat, Baldwin renamed the organization the Civil Liberties Bureau. It didn't help. Since Roger refused to tone down his rhetoric and calm down his activity, the AUAM decided on October 1, 1917 to sever all ties with both him and the Bureau. So, once again the organization was renamed and reincorporated — this time as the National Civil Liberties Bureau.

But that was just the beginning of Roger's troubles. One of the first pieces of literature that he wrote for the new Bureau was declared "unmailable" by the Post Office because of its "radical and subversive views." A short while later, the Bureau's offices were raided by the FBI and its files confiscated. And if that weren't enough, twelve days later Roger was called to register for the draft.

True to form, Roger decided to resist the draft, and he was promptly arrested and brought to trial. Before the bench, he unashamedly professed his commitment to Anarchism, his association with the IWW, and his allegiance to Socialistic Reform. And though his forthrightness won for him the admiration of the judge, it did not clear him of his offense. He was sentenced to a year in the penitentiary. Emma Goldman said then, that he had "proved himself the most consistent" of all the reformers, and that she was "prouder of him" than of anyone else.[20]

While he was imprisoned, Roger relaxed and caught up on his reading. But more importantly, he began to work seriously on his relationship with Madeline Doty, a well known writer whom he had been casually dating for some time. By the time he was released, they were completely "in love," and less than a month later, they were married.

The wedding was a very progressive affair — outdoors, casual dress, no ring, and no religious symbolism. Even the vows Roger wrote for the occasion reflected their radicalism:

> The highest relationship between a man and a woman is that which welcomes and understands each other's loves. Without a sense of possession there can be no exclusions, no jealousies. The creative life demands many friendships, many loves shared together openly, honestly, and joyously. Our primary interest and joy is the great revolutionary struggle for human freedom today, so intense, so full of promise. We regard our union as only contributing to that *cause*, making us both serve it the more passionately, the more devotedly.[21]

This model "open" marriage was to be lived on a "fifty-fifty basis." Each was to be responsible for their own expenses, and Madeline was to keep her own name — as Roger said, "I am unalterably opposed to any woman taking my name. It's all I've got to identify me, and I am not going to give it away to a woman."[22]

A marriage set on such a foundation is sure to run into trouble. And indeed, it was not long before their marital bliss became merely an expression in the ether, like the smirk of the Cheshire Cat.

Roger grew up in an unhappy home, and he somehow made certain that the rest of his life would be little different. He quashed his new love, rushing along the downgrade of adultery, separation, betrayal, divorce, remarriage, and the tragic suicide of a spurned child.

After only two months, Roger left Madeline and "went on the bum" joining the IWW as a common laborer. He wanted to do what neither Marx nor Lenin—nor for that matter, any of the other "champions" of the proletariat—had done: actually *work* among the people he was hoping to one day "liberate." He traveled around almost aimlessly, shoveling iron ore at a steel mill, loading raw materials in a brick yard, and laboring on a railroad construction crew.

As admirable as his desires were, hard physical work was a bit much for a Boston Brahmin. After three months, Roger gave up his adventure and returned home. Recalling his perambulations later, he would echo Clarence Darrow's remark saying that, "I'd rather be the friend of the workingman than be the workingman: it's a lot easier."[23]

And so, having failed at being "one of them," he settled on being "one with them."

Sovietization

Upon his return, Roger set about trying to salvage what was left of his Civil Liberties Bureau. It had struggled along without him for more than a year and was virtually inoperative. On January 20, 1920, he moved it into new offices on West Thirteenth Street in New York—shared with the Communist Party's *New Masses* tabloid. He also reincorporated and renamed it for the third and final time.

The new American Civil Liberties Union was to serve the various subversive and revolutionary labor movements to which Anna Louise Strong, Margaret Sanger, and Emma Goldman had convinced him to dedicate his life. There was no pretense of objectivity. "The *cause* we now serve is labor,"

Roger wrote in a memo at the time. "We are frankly partisans of labor in the present struggle."[24]

The ACLU was not Roger's only contribution to radicalism, however. In 1920 he also launched the Mutual Aid Society to offer financial help to "Leftist intellectuals, trade unionists, and the radical fringe."[25] He started the International Committee for Political Prisoners to provide counsel and support to Anarchist and Communist subversives who had been deported for their criminal activities. He helped to establish the American Fund for Public Service — with two million dollars donated by Charles Garland a rich young radical from Boston — in order to pour vast sums of money into revolutionary causes. And finally, he developed close institutional ties with "the Communist movement and the Socialist International."

Roger had by this time moved fully into the orbit of Soviet admirers, and he earnestly desired to see a Bolshevik insurgency in America. He wrote that Lenin's totalitarian regime was "the greatest and most daring experiment yet undertaken to recreate society in terms of human values." He went on to say that it was "a great laboratory of social experiment of incalculable value to the development of the world."[26]

In his book *Liberty Under the Soviets*, written after a blissful visit to Russia, Roger admitted that the government there had instituted "complete censorship of all means of communications and the complete suppression of any organized opposition to the dictatorship or its program."[27] He went on to state that "no civil liberty as we understand it in the West exists for the opponents of the regime."[28] Despite this, he lauded the Soviet State for the "far more significant freedom of workers," the "abolition of the privileged classes," the "revolution in education," and the "liberty won for anti-religion."[29]

How did this "champion" of civil liberties justify such seeming contradictions in his values? Very simply, he baptized the facts with his ideology:

Such an attitude as I express toward the relation of economic to civil liberty may easily be construed as condoning in Russia repressions which I condemn in Capitalist countries. It is true that I feel differently about them, because they are unlike. Repressions in Western Democracies are violations of professed constitutional liberties, and I condemn them as such. Repressions in Soviet Russia are the weapons of struggle in a transition period to Socialism.[30]

Like so many liberals, Roger had twenty-twenty vision in his right eye, but was blind in his left.

In an article he wrote for *Soviet Russia Today*, he again utterly contradicted his professed concerns with civil liberties for the sake of ideology saying, "When the power of the working class is once achieved, as it has been only in the Soviet Union, I am for maintaining it by any means whatever," And again, "No champion of a Socialist society could fail to see that some suppression was necessary to achieve it."[31]

To work in solidarity with his comrades, Roger joined scores of "United Front" organizations. Many years later, in 1976, he would admit that they were essentially "recruiting centers" for the Communist Party where "lists could be taken, sympathizers spotted and enrolled, and funds could be siphoned off for Party purposes." He said:

I joined. I don't regret being a part of the Communist tactic which increased the effectiveness of a good *cause*. I knew what I was doing. I was not an innocent liberal. I wanted what the Communists wanted and I traveled the United Front road to get it.[32]

The work of the ACLU naturally reflected this Sovietization. Of the ACLU Board and National Committee members elected during the first sixty years of the organization, almost eighty percent had Communist affiliations.[33] A full ninety percent of the cases that it defended involved Communists.[34] And as a result, it was stigmatized as a "Communist-Front" organization itself.[35] It came under investigation of the House Un-American Activities Committee.[36] It was lambasted in the press as a subversive threat to the security of the nation.[37] And it was even isolated from the mainstream labor movement and the more moderate liberal reform organizations.[38]

Roger seemed entirely unconcerned with the controversy. In a letter to Emma Goldman he wrote, "I see so much to be said for the destruction of privilege based on wealth that I will stand for Russia against the rest of the world."[39]

But, his edenic allegiance was suddenly spoiled on August 20, 1939. It was then that Roger's greatest hero, Josef Stalin, signed a non-aggression pact with Roger's greatest nemesis, Adolf Hitler. In a jolt, the ancient apartheid of Yankee fastidiousness separated him from the object of his devotion. In a single stroke, the urbane veneer had slipped from Soviet intentions. Roger at last realized that the emperor had no clothes.

Legitimization

"Hell hath no fury," says Dick Gregory, "like a liberal scorned."[40] Immediately, Roger moved to publicly distance himself and the ACLU from the Communist Party and the various Front organizations that he had been a part of for so long. He even moved to purge the Board of any Party members. He made a herculean effort to legitimize the work of civil liberties in the eyes of the establishment. It was not that his political and philosophical beliefs had changed. He was as committed to the *cause* as ever. It was just that the Soviet betrayal had made him a bit more realistic—and a good deal more pragmatic. He focused once again on the courts—as opposed to international politics—as the best and surest path to radical reform. Instead of subverting the moral order of the nation and its institutions openly through revolution, he draped his subterfuge in the rhetoric and aura of constitutionalism, liberty, and patriotism. He explained this new ruse in a letter to his Communist friend Louis Lochner:

We want to look like patriots in everything we do. We want to get a lot of flags, talk a great deal about the Constitution and what our forefathers wanted to make of this country and to show that we are the fellows that really stand for the spirit of our institutions.[41]

This new moderated public relations image proved to be a very effective strategy—of course, the fact that under FDR, the government was actively sponsoring a variety Leftist causes didn't hurt either. By the end of the Second World War, the ACLU was accepted into the mainstream. One of its members—Felix Frankfurter—had been elevated to the Supreme Court, and another—Francis Biddle—had even become the U.S. Attorney General. Later, the Truman, Eisenhower, Kennedy, Johnson, and Carter Administrations would literally be filled with high-level ACLU members and supporters. The rehabilitation was complete.

In short order, the ACLU and its founder were lionized and tenured in the hallowed halls of the American Establishment—keeping company with any number of other once disreputable *causes, faiths,* and *movements:* Planned Parenthood, the National Organization of Women, the Council on Foreign Relations, the Trilateral Commission, and the National Education Association among many others. In one of his final actions as President in 1981, Jimmy Carter awarded Roger the Medal of Freedom—the nation's highest civilian honor.

"We learn from experience, " George Bernard Shaw said, "that men never learn anything from experience."[42] That is why Trojan Horses always work.

Conclusion

In his remarkable book *The Foes of Our Own Household,* written in 1918, Theodore Roosevelt argued that:

There are dreadful woes in modern life, dreadful suffering among some of those who toil, brutal wrong-doing among some of those who make colossal fortunes by exploiting the toilers. It is the duty of every honest and upright man, of every man who holds within his breast the capacity for righteous indignation, to recognize these wrongs, and to strive with all his might to bring about a better condition of things. But he will never bring about this better condition by misstating facts and advocating remedies which are not merely false, but fatal.[43]

There can be no doubt that there have been — and continue to be — civil liberties violations in this country. But there can also be no doubt that the ACLU was never — and is not now — the solution to that unhappy reality. To claim otherwise is to misstate facts and to advocate remedies which are not merely false, but fatal.

The ACLU is the legal branch of an ideological cult that is utterly and completely inimical to the American system of truth and justice. It is, in short, a purloined conscience.

PART THREE

THE ISSUES

Note that pendants lose all proportion. They never can keep sane in a discussion. They will go wild on matters they are wholly unable to judge. Never do they use one of those three phrases which keep a man steady and balance his mind; I mean the words (1) After all it is not my business. (2) Tut! Tut! You don't say so! And (3) Credo in Unum Deum Patrem Omnipotentem, Factorem omnium visibilium atque invisibilium; in which last, there is a power of synthesis that can jam all their analytical dust-heap into such a fine, tight, and compact body as would make them stare to see.[1]

Hilaire Belloc

What is now called free thought is valued, not because it is free thought, but because it is freedom from thought; because it is free thoughtlessness.[2]

G.K. Chesterton

5

RELIGIOUS
EXPRESSION

qui lundit in cathedra, lugebit in gehenna[3]

It is not difficult to discern that the practical man in social reform is exactly the same animal as the practical man in every other department of human energy, and may be discovered suffering from the same twin disabilities which stamp the practical man wherever found: an inability to define his own first principles and an inability to follow the consequences proceeding from his own action.[4]

Hilaire Belloc

The enemies of religion cannot leave it alone. They laboriously attempt to smash religion. They cannot smash religion; but they do smash everything else.[5]

G.K. Chesterton

When it comes to the Christian faith, the spokesmen, policy-makers, and attorneys for the ACLU have made their position painfully clear: they're against it. No *ifs*, *ands*, or *buts* about it.

Although they have fought for the free speech and expression "rights" of pornographers, witches, abortionists, homosexuals, convicted criminals, child molesters, occultists, Communists, lesbians, Nazis, illegal aliens, AIDS patients, and Satanists, they have resolutely attempted to deny those same privileges to Christians. As a result, according to Richard and Susan Vigilante, they have effectively reduced "the place of religion in American life" and have restricted religious speech "in a way they would never allow other forms of speech to be restricted."[6]

Their discriminatory intolerance is a matter of record.[7] Recently, they have sought to:

- Halt the singing of Christmas carols like "Silent Night" and "Away in a Manger" in public facilities;

- Deny the tax-exempt status of all churches — yet maintaining it for themselves as well as for various occult groups;

- Disallow prayer — not just in the public school classrooms, but in locker rooms, sports arenas, graduation exercises, and legislative assemblies;

- Terminate all military and prison chaplains;

- Deny Christian school children access to publicly funded services;

- Eliminate nativity scenes, crosses, and other Christian symbols from public property;

- Repeal all blue law statutes;

- Prohibit voluntary Bible reading in public schools — even during free time or after classes;

- Remove the words *In God We Trust* from our coins;

- Deny accreditation to science departments at Bible-believing Christian Universities;

- Prevent the posting of the Ten Commandments in classrooms;

- Terminate all voucher programs and tuition tax credits;

- Prohibit census questions about religious affiliation;

- Purge the words *under God* from the Pledge of Allegiance.

As Patrick Buchanan has all too obviously pointed out, "That is not a record of tolerance."[8]

Interestingly, the ACLU is led into this absurd contradiction of its stated purpose because it sees the Christian faith as "an almost irresistible persuasive force."[9] Gadfly liberal columnist Nat Hentoff has said that the ACLU seems to be "afraid of making religious speech first-class speech, the way all other speech is" because it really ascribes "extraordinary powers to religious speech."[10] In other words, the ACLU fears Christianity in a way that it fears nothing else.

Of course, its fear is cloaked in high-sounding Constitutional concerns—its bigotry is not overly blatant. It makes much ado over the principle of "separation of church and state." It brandishes the idea of "the wall of separation" like a saber. And it fixates on the "establishment clause" of the First Amendment. According to Barry Lynn, the ACLU's Legislative Director:

There is clearly a distinction made between religious speech and activity and any other speech and activity. . . . There is an establishment clause which limits and tempers only religious speech and activity. There is no establishment clause which in any way limits economic, cultural, historical, or philosophical expression. Thus, the state may embrace any economic, political, or philosophical theory; it may not embrace or enhance any religious activity.[11]

Thus, according to the ACLU, the Christian faith is so powerful, so dangerous, and so intrusive that the founding fathers had to design the Constitution in order to protect us from it. Despite the fact that such a reading of history is con-voluted at best, the ACLU has been very successful in press-ing it upon our courts, schools, and communities all across the country. For all intents and purposes, says Russell Kirk, it has been able to "harass out of existence" public expressions of faith.[12]

Separation of Church and State

The ACLU's almost Bolshevik understanding of the sepa-ration of church and state was by no means shared by America's framers. In fact, they readily admitted that their new nation was utterly dependent upon a Christian social order — and its incumbent Christian influences. America was founded as a Christian nation.

Joseph Story, the foremost historian of the founding era, underscored this truth in his book, *Commentaries on the Con-stitution*, published in 1833:

The First Amendment was not intended to withdraw the Christian religion as a whole from the protection of Con-gress. At the time, the general if not universal sentiment in America was, that Christianity ought to receive encourage-ment from the state so far as was compatible with the pri-vate rights of conscience and the freedom of worship. Any attempt to level all religions, and to make it a matter of state policy to hold all in utter indifference would have created universal indignation.[13]

More than a century later liberal Supreme Court Justice William O. Douglas reaffirmed that historical verity:

> We are a religious people whose institutions presuppose a Supreme Being. We guarantee the freedom to worship as one chooses. We make room for as wide a variety of beliefs and creeds as the spiritual needs of man deem necessary. We sponsor an attitude on the part of government that shows no partiality to any one group and that lets each flourish according to the zeal of its adherents and the appeal of its dogma. When the state encourages religious instruction or cooperates with religious authorities by adjusting the schedule of public events to sectarian needs, it follows the best of our traditions. For it then respects the religious nature of our people and accommodates the public service to their spiritual needs. To hold that it may not, would be to find in the Constitution a requirement that the government show a callous indifference to religious groups. That would be preferring those who believe in no religion over those who do believe. We find no such Constitutional requirement which makes it necessary for government to be hostile to religion and to throw its weight against efforts to widen the effective scope of religious influence.[14]

Justice Douglas went on to assert without hesitation that, "The First Amendment does not say that in every and all respects there shall be a separation of church and state."[15]

It is true that the Founding Fathers designed the Constitution to clearly differentiate between church and state. There was to be no intermingling. They were to be separate institutions — with separate jurisdictions, separate authorities, and separate functions. They knew that a Christian social order depends on this kind of distinction. When any one institution begins to encroach upon another, chaos and tyranny inevitably result. The Biblical notion of checks and balances begins to break down. They knew that from personal experience.

Thus, they made certain that the state could not meddle in the affairs of the church. The church was to be outside the state's jurisdiction. This really is the force of the First Amendment: "Congress shall make no law respecting an establishment of religion, or prohibiting the free exercise thereof." The state has no authority over the church and therefore was not to regulate, impede, or interfere in its work. Local municipalities and even individual commonwealths were free to render support to the church—as often they did—but never were they to have control over it. Certainly they were never to gag the church in the manner the ACLU has sought to gag it.

The framers also wanted to make certain that the church did not meddle in the affairs of the state. The state was to be outside the church's jurisdiction. They wanted to protect their fledgling Republic from any and all tyrannies. They wanted to avoid *statism*—in the form of imperialism, socialism, or even democracy. And they wanted to avoid *oligarchy*—in the form of caesaro-papism, agathism, or even ecclesiocracy.

Even so, this did not mean that they wanted to ensure that church and state had *nothing* to do with each other. On the contrary, they simply wanted to clear the way for church and state to cooperate with each other in building a Christian cultural consensus. Church and state were to balance one another. They were to serve one another. They were to check one another. They were to encourage one another. In other words, the founding fathers never envisioned a "wall of separation." Instead, they saw church and state as distinct but cooperative and interdependent.

The state was to protect the church with just laws and a righteous restraint upon the citizenry so that the Gospel could do its work in peace and harmony. The state was to do and facilitate good deeds and encourage social enhancement.

The church on the other hand, was to teach the Bible—the common standard of law for both church and state. It was to mobilize the forces of mercy, truth, and justice. And it was to expose sin, encourage the magistrates, and train the people.

The framers thus set up the American system as a decentralized, confederated, and self-consciously Christian social structure. It followed the Biblical order of multiple jurisdictions, separate but cooperating, under the sovereignty of God and the rule of His law.

That is a far cry from the ACLU version of Constitutional law.

But the facts are inescapable. Throughout our early history, the necessity of a free and expressive Christian witness was shared by all our great leaders:

- George Washington, the hero of the Revolution and the first President under the Constitution, added the pledge, "So help me God," to his inaugural oath, and then stooped to kiss the Bible as an affirmation of his submission to the King of kings and Lord of lords. He later asserted, "It is impossible to rightly govern the world without God and the Bible."[16]

- John Adams, the second President, made no secret of the fact that he studied the Bible often and with diligence in order to discern the proper administration of a Christian society. He said, "Our Constitution was made only for a moral and religious people. So great is my veneration of the Bible that the earlier my children begin to read it, the more confident will be my hope that they will prove useful citizens of their country and respectful members of society."[17]

- Thomas Jefferson, the primary author of the Declaration of Independence and the third President, was also quite forthright in his acknowledgement of the necessity of a Christian foundation for this Republic. He said, "The Bible is the cornerstone of liberty. A student's perusal of the sacred volume will make him a better citizen, a better father, a better husband."[18]

• Benjamin Franklin, the patriarch of the Constitutional Convention, said, "A nation of well informed men who have been taught to know the price of the rights which God has given them, cannot be enslaved."[19]

• Andrew Jackson, the country's seventh President, read the Bible daily, and often referred to it as "the Rock on which our Republic rests."[20]

• Noah Webster, the great author, educator, and lexicographer said that, "The moral principles and precepts contained in the Scriptures form the basis of all our civil constitution and laws. All the miseries and evils which other nations suffer from vice, crime, ambition, injustice, oppression, slavery, and war, proceed from their despising or neglecting the precepts contained in the Bible."[21]

• Abraham Lincoln, President of the Union during the tumultuous days of the War Between the States, called the Bible "the best Gift God has ever given to man. . . . But for it we could not know right from wrong."[22] He went on to say that, "It is the duty of nations, as well as of men, to own their dependence upon the overruling power of God and to recognize the sublime truth announced in the Holy Scriptures and proven by all history, that those nations only are blessed whose God is the Lord."[23]

• U.S. Grant, the hero of Appomattox and eighteenth President, enjoined his fellow citizens to "Hold fast to the Bible as the sheet-anchor of your liberties; write its precepts in your hearts and practice them in your lives. To the influence of this book we are indebted for all the progress made in true civilization and to this we must look as our guide in the future."[24]

- Theodore Roosevelt, the paradigm of American patriotism and President at the turn of the century said, "In this actual world, a churchless community, a community where men have abandoned and scoff at, or ignore their Christian duties, is a community on the rapid down-grade."[25]

Notice, that many of these men were not themselves orthodox Christians. Adams and Jefferson were Unitarians, and Franklin was a deist. But each of them understood the importance of integrating the Christian faith into the fabric of society if the great American experiment of freedom and liberty were to succeed in any measure. They did not—and in fact, could not—imagine a separation between faith and polity, between individual morality and civic morality.

Even if the voices of those great men were silenced by the subverters of our history, the rocks and stones themselves would cry out. In our public buildings, irrefutable evidence of our country's Christian heritage abounds: the Ten Commandments hang over the head of the Chief Justice in the Supreme Court; in the House and Senate chambers appear the words, *In God We Trust*; in the capitol rotunda is the figure of the crucified Christ; carvings on the capitol dome testify to, "The New Testament according to the Lord and Savior Jesus Christ"; the Great Seal of the United States proclaims, "*Annuit Coeptis*," which means, "God has smiled on our undertaking"; under the seal is inscribed the phrase from Lincoln's Gettysburg Address, "This nation under God"; the walls of the Library of Congress are adorned with the words of Psalm 19:1 and Micah 6:8; engraved on the metal cap of the Washington Monument are the words, *Praise be to God*; and lining the stairwell are numerous Scripture verses that apply the

Christian faith to every sphere of life from the family to business, from personal character to government.[26]

The men who built this nation knew what we must know: that America depended upon Christianity for its founding, and that it shall ever depend upon it for its perpetuation.

Conclusion

According to Russell Kirk, "True law is rooted in ethical assumptions or norms; and those moral principles are derived, in the beginning at least, from religious convictions."[27] In the United States, the religious convictions upon which our law is based are Christian. That means that if we attack public expressions of the Christian faith — as the ACLU would have us to do — we actually attack our very foundations of justice and liberty. If we institutionalize hostility to Christianity we instigate a riotous revolution which can only undermine the entire culture.

The issue of church-state relations is not so much one of civil liberty, toleration, and justice as it is one of survival — the survival of Western Civilization in general and of American Culture in particular.

As George Washington so aptly and prophetically asserted:

Morality is the necessary spring of popular government. And let us with caution indulge the supposition that morality can be maintained without Christianity. Whatever may be conceded to the influence of refined education on minds of peculiar structure, reason and experience both forbid us to expect that national morality can prevail in exclusion of religious principle.[28]

6

ABORTION, INFANTICIDE, AND EUTHANASIA

hic se aperit diabolis[1]

The accursed everyday life of the modernist is instinct with the four sins crying to heaven for vengeance, and there is no humanity in it, and no simplicity, and no recollection.[2]

Hilaire Belloc

The worship of will is the negation of will. To admire mere choice is to refuse to choose. You cannot admire will in general, because the essence of will is that it is particular. Every act of will is an act of self-limitation. To desire action is to desire limitation. In that sense every act is an act of self-sacrifice. When you choose anything you reject everything else.[3]

G.K. Chesterton

The ACLU is an unapologetic advocate of abortion on demand.[4] It argues for its unregulated permissibility even after a child has reached what medical theorists call the "point of viability."[5] In addition, it freely supports the perpetuation of infanticide.[6] And it openly lobbies for the liberalization of euthanasia laws.[7]

Very simply, the organization is at the forefront of the legal battle over the sanctity of human life. It has handled more than seventy percent of all medical ethics cases in U.S. courts.[8] It has participated, in one way or another, in every abortion case that has appeared before the Supreme Court.[9] And it has been unyielding in its insistence that the government provide the medical atrocities of abortion, infanticide, and euthanasia as a service to all citizens out of the tax largess.[10]

In every respect, the ACLU toes the liberal party line — even in the face of blatant contradictions with its own civil liberties principles and moral rhetoric. And those contradictions abound:

- It has said that it "condemns" any "lack of respect for human life."[11]

- It says that it abhors anything that might "give society the unmistakable message that life ceases to be sacred when it is thought useful to take it and that violence is legitimate when it is thought justified by pragmatic concerns that appeal to those having the legal power to kill."[12]

- It argues that, "A civilized and humane society does not deliberately kill human beings."[13]

- It asserts that teaching "the permissibility of killing people to solve social problems is the worst possible example to set for any society."[14]

Its own ardent pro-life rhetoric notwithstanding, the ACLU has maintained its unequivocal pro-death position ever since Roger Baldwin (the ACLU's founder and leading light) and Margaret Sanger (Planned Parenthood's founder and leading light) first became comrades-in-arms, back in

1915. This irony is never reconciled in its literature. Instead, the official *ACLU Policy Guide* ambiguously states that the organization can offer "no comment on the wisdom or the moral implications" of pro-death activities, arguing that such matters fall into the nether realm of "free speech and privacy rights." Accordingly, over the years the ACLU has sought to:[15]

- Abrogate all state and local laws regulating abortion trafficking — even before the *Roe v. Wade* and *Doe v. Bolton* cases were heard before the Supreme Court;

- Require states to effect "living will" statutes legalizing "consensual mercy killing" for the "terminally ill or permanently disabled";

- Ban "informed consent" requirements that would inform women of the many medical risks inherent to abortion procedures and allow them to have access to information about fetal development;

- Decriminalize "assisted suicide";

- Deregulate abortion procedures through the entire nine months of gestation — making abortion the only completely unregulated surgical procedure in all of medicine;

- Disallow spousal consent laws;

- Disallow parental consent laws;

- Refuse even parental notice requirements;

- Oppose regulations that require reasonable and humane treatment of the children that survive abortion procedures;

- Require Federal, state, and local funding for abortion and birth limitation services for all citizens;

- Coordinate its judicial, legislative, and educational efforts with Planned Parenthood, the Hemlock Society, the National Abortion Rights Action League, the National Abortion Federation, the Alan Guttmacher Institute, and other radical pro-death advocacy groups.

These judicial demands are claimed as "basic civil rights" and "fundamental civil liberties" for women, the terminally ill, or the permanently disabled. Of course, the ACLU somehow fails to mention the civil liberties concerns of the children that are ripped limb from limb inside their mothers' wombs, or are starved to death in the neo-natal wards of our hospitals, or are drowned in poisonous solutions, or are experimented on in research laboratories, or have their organs harvested from their bodies one by one. It also fails to mention the civil liberties concerns of parents, spouses, communities, and tax paying citizens who are forced into a position of either helpless complicity or total incognizance by its pro-death policies.

And as if all that were not bad enough, the ACLU takes its pro-death commitment one step further still: actually enjoining civil liberties sanctions on pro-life groups that oppose abortion, infanticide, and euthanasia. It seems that some civil liberties are guaranteed by the First Amendment only to those citizens that happen to agree with the ACLU's liberal worldview and social agenda. For instance:

- Though the *Policy Guide* says that, "The ACLU supports the right to picket in any circumstances, by any method, and in any numbers," it has often fought to limit the circumstances, methods, and numbers for peaceful pro-life protests.[16]

- The ACLU officially deplores espionage tactics in all other circumstances and situations, but when it comes to pro-life protesters, it condones implementing special surveillance measures, compiling dossiers on individuals, and photographing "potential" opponents for later litigation.[17]

- Despite the fact that it says that, "Orderly, non-violent protests such as sit-ins are not a trespass on private property but rather a constitutional right to express opinion," pro-life rescuers have been consistently denied that right—and the ACLU has advised abortion chambers to dogmatically enforce trespassing "violations."[18]

- It has often defended anti-war, nuclear, and ecology protesters when they have crossed state lines to "incite riots," but in the case of peaceful pro-life protesters, it has advised the enforcement of Federal racketeering statutes—or RICO laws.[19]

Thus, as a result of its foursquare commitment to the pro-death ideology, the ACLU has been forced to contradict not only its carefully phrased moral rhetoric, but its most cherished and fundamental principles as well.

Even that though, is not the worst of it. The most serious consequence of the ACLU's advocacy of death on demand, is its affront to the rule of law.

Law and Life

The great liberties that we enjoy in America have been secured against the arbitrary and fickle whims of men and movements by the rule of law. Our system of government does not depend upon the benevolence of the magistrates, or the altruism of the wealthy, or the condescension of the powerful. Every citizen, rich or poor, man or woman, native-born or immigrant, hale or handicapped, young or old, is equal under the standard of unchanging, immutable, and impartial justice.

As Thomas Paine wrote in *Common Sense*, the powerful booklet that helped spark the War for Independence, "In America, the law is king."[20]

If left to the mere discretion of human authorities, statutes, edicts, and ordinances inevitably devolve into tyranny. There must, therefore, be an absolute against which no encroachment of prejudice or preference may interfere. There must be a foundation that the winds of change and the waters of circumstance cannot erode. There must be a basis for law that can be depended upon at all times, in all places, and in every situation.

Apart from this Christian innovation in the affairs of men, there can be no freedom. There never has been before, and there never will be again. Our founding fathers knew that only too well.

The opening refrain of the Declaration of Independence affirms the necessity of an absolute standard upon which the rule of law must be based:

> We hold these truths to be self-evident, that all men are created equal; that they are endowed by their Creator with certain inalienable rights; that among these are life, liberty, and the pursuit of happiness. That, to secure these rights, governments are instituted among men, deriving their just powers from the consent of the governed.

Appealing to the "Supreme Judge of the World" for guidance, and relying on His "Divine Providence" for wisdom, the framers committed themselves and their posterity to the absolute standard of "the laws of nature and nature's God." And the essence of that standard, they said, were the inalienable, God-given, and sovereignly endowed rights of *life, liberty,* and *the pursuit of happiness.* A just government exists, they argued, solely and completely to "provide guards" for the "future security" of that essence. Take it away, and the rule of law is no longer possible.

Thomas Jefferson asserted that "the chief purpose of government is to protect life. Abandon that and you have abandoned all."[21]

Abraham Lincoln pressed the same issue home when he questioned the institution of slavery on the basis of the sanctity of all human life and the rule of law:

> I should like to know if taking this old Declaration of Independence, which declares that all men are equal upon principle, and making exceptions to it, where it will stop. If one man says it does not mean a Negro, why not another say it does not mean some other man?[22]

Because the ACLU — and its pro-death bedfellows — have been so diligent in their assault on the unborn, the aged, and the infirmed, the rule of law in our land is now in real jeopardy. No one is absolutely secure, because absoluteness has been thrown out of our constitutional vocabulary. Now that the right to life has been abrogated for at least some citizens, *all* the liberties of *all* the citizens are at risk because suddenly arbitrariness, relativism, and randomness have entered the legal equation. The checks against petty partiality and blatant bias have been disabled.

This is not the rule of law. It is the brutal imposition of fashion and fancy by privileged interlopers.

Ronald Reagan in his book, *Abortion and the Conscience of the Nation*, pointed out that, "Our nation-wide policy of abortion on demand through all nine months of pregnancy was neither voted for by our people nor enacted by our legislators — not a single state had such unrestricted abortion before the Supreme Court decreed it to be national policy in 1973."[23] The pro-death stance of the court was, he said, "an act of raw judicial power."[24] It was a denial of the rule of law. It was a tyrannical usurpation of life, liberty, and the pursuit of happiness because, as the President said, "We cannot di-

minish the value of one category of human life — the unborn — without diminishing the value of all human life."[25]

Although these truths are "self-evident" in the sense that
they are written on the fleshly tablet of every man's heart,
they are by no means universally accepted (see Romans 1:19–
22). In fact, such reasoning is to some a "stumbling block"
and to others "mere foolishness" (see 1 Corinthians 1:23).
That is because the rule of law is a Christian idea, made possible only by the revelation of law from on high. And all too
many men "suppress" that truth in one way, shape, form, or
another (see Romans 1:18).

Thomas Jefferson acknowledged this saying:

> Can the liberties of a nation be sure when we remove their
> only firm basis, a conviction in the minds of the people, that
> these liberties are the gift of God? That they are not to be
> violated but with His wrath? Indeed, I tremble for my coun-
> try, when I reflect that God is just; that His justice cannot
> sleep forever, that revolution of the wheel of fortune, a
> change of situation, is among possible events; that it may be-
> come probable by supernatural influence! The Almighty has
> no attribute which can take side with us in that event.[26]

In order to protect and preserve *any* rights we must protect and preserve *all* rights — beginning with the fundamental
rights of life, liberty, and the pursuit of happiness. But in order
to protect *those* rights, we must return to that distinctly Christian notion that the God who providentially rules the affairs of
men has already inalienably endowed them to each of us.

Conclusion

Theodore Roosevelt, writing on the eve of America's
entry into the First World War in 1917, exhorted his fellow
citizens to be on guard against the erosion of the rule of law:

The world is at this moment passing through one of those terrible periods of convulsion when the souls of men and of nations are tried as by fire. Woe to the man or to the nation that at such a time stands as once Laodicea stood; as the people of ancient Meroz stood, when they dared not come to the help of the Lord against the mighty. In such a crisis the moral weakling is the enemy of the right, the enemy of life, liberty, and the pursuit of happiness.[27]

Apparently, we are once again passing through one of those terrible periods of convulsion. Surely the souls of men and of nations are being tried as by fire. Life, liberty, and the pursuit of happiness are at risk as in no other time in our history. The ACLU and other advocates of death on demand and arbitrary law now pose a threat, not just to the unborn, the aged, and the infirmed, but to us all.

This was the very thing that Thomas Jefferson most feared when he implored the citizens of America to cling to the absolute standard of law, saying, "Our peculiar security is in the possession of a written Constitution. Let us not make it a blank paper by construction."[28]

Our best hope for civil liberties protection in the future is not the ACLU. It is a return to the rule of law based on the inalienable right to life endowed to all men by their Creator. May we not be like the Laodiceans in the present struggle to effect that return.

7

PORNOGRAPHY AND PERVERSION

manet lex tota pietatis[1]

One can only say to ancient sophistical difficulties, that the sense of men establishes for itself the true limits of any object, as of freedom.[2]

Hilaire Belloc

It is not natural or obvious to let a man utter follies and abominations any more than it is natural or obvious to let a man dig up part of the public road, or infect half a town with typhoid fever. The principle of free speech is that truth is so much larger and stranger and many-sided than we know of, that it is very much better at all costs to hear every one's account of it.[3]

G.K. Chesterton

An avalanche of perversity has crashed over our land in recent years laying waste nearly everything in its path. The problems of pornography, infidelity, homosexuality, prostitution, and promiscuity have begun to significantly erode the stability of our cultural foundations:

- Pornography has become a frighteningly powerful multi-billion dollar a year industry in the U.S. — with higher sales figures than even *McDonald's*.[4]

- It has, in fact, become the fastest growing segment of the American "entertainment" industry.[5]

- With its very clear connections with violent crime, organized crime, and societal dysfunction, all of the various manifestations of pornography — soft porn, hard porn, child porn, violent porn, live porn, video porn, phone porn, cable porn, peep porn, snuff porn, audio porn, glitz porn, pulp porn, and slick porn — are dangerous incursions on the security and liberty of us all.[6]

- Infidelity has reached epidemic proportions in our society. Recent surveys indicate that as many as seventy-five percent of all men and sixty-five percent of all women violate the sanctity of their marriage covenants at one time or another — thus partly explaining why an astonishing two-thirds of all family units are fractured by separation and divorce.[7]

- Is it any wonder then that a full fifty-four percent of all Americans believe the family is disappearing from American life?[8]

- Homosexuality has come out of the closet, marched through our communities, ravaged our young, and checked into the hospital. Unnatural relations between men and men or women and women was once considered "a psychosis" and "a threat to the health of the nation."[9] But now, even though millions of people are literally dying due to its twisted compulsions and filthy passions, homosexuality is being conferred a privileged "minority" status — thus propagating its contagion all the more.[10]

- Prostitution, like pornography, is becoming an ever more dominant factor in the economic ecology of our nation. With the proliferation of bath houses, massage parlors, escort services, nude bars and swank bordellos in virtually every region and locale, the once seedy and shadowy profession has been transformed into a far-flung multi-million dollar a year modern industry—in many places legal, in most others, unregulated and unchecked.[11]

- Unchecked promiscuity now runs rampant. The "sexual revolution" of the sixties and seventies has come and gone, leaving in its wake innumerable casualties—as all revolutions are wont to do. Recent studies indicate that the residual damage is even worse than what we might expect. Only thirty-one percent of American women wait until marriage before engaging in sexual relations.[12] Only twenty percent of men do.[13] Forty-three percent of all teens under the age of seventeen have already initiated sexual activity.[14]

- Perhaps we should not be surprised then that more than half of all marriages in America today fail within the first seven years—they are on shaky ground before they even begin.[15]

In the midst of this awful conflagration of crises stands the ACLU. But instead of defending the integrity of our families, the viability our community standards, and the efficacy of our cultural consensus against the onslaught of immorality, it has taken the other side. It has, in fact, dedicated itself to proselytize for perversity at every opportunity and on every occasion. Accordingly, over the years the organization has sought to:[16]

- Legalize the distribution of all pornography—including violent, degrading, bestial, and child pornography;

- Abrogate community standards restrictions on all forms of obscenity;

- Afford unrestricted access to the mails for pornographers;

- Remove all media ethics standards for radio, television, and cable broadcasts;

- Disallow any and all rating codes for movies and videos;

- Decriminalize all homosexual activities;

- Deregulate bath houses, nude bars, massage parlors, and peep shows;

- Provide homosexuals with a privileged "minority" status as a legally enforceable civil right—thus granting them preferential hiring and advancement treatment in the business marketplace;

- Grant AIDS sufferers a legal "disability" status—thus bequeathing them with a vast array of tax paid entitlements;

- Hinder health department attempts to contain sexually transmitted diseases on the basis of the "right to privacy";

- Legalize prostitution;

- Allow open and profligate sexual solicitation in public places;

- Develop a close partnership between itself, the public sector, and Planned Parenthood in encouraging teen sexual activity through indoctrination with lurid sexuality awareness courses, providing youngsters with contraceptive devices without parental consent or approval, and encouraging women to take advantage of the burgeoning and wildly profitable abortion trade;

- Disallow the enforcement of the marriage covenant as a binding legal contract;

- And, remove all sanctions against the disruption of the marriage covenant.

Even taking into consideration the organization's cozy and lucrative relationship with the Playboy Foundation,[17] its advocacy of such concupiscent causes is difficult to fathom. Who but the ACLU could actually defend child pornography? Or brutal and demeaning violent pornography? Or the relaxation of health precautions in the midst of the AIDS plague? Or further exacerbation of the teen pregnancy epidemic? Or the complete legalization and deregulation of prostitution? Even the most libertine and leftist politicos recognize that such nefarious depravity is detrimental to the nation's vitality.

But, according to the ACLU, each of these issues falls into the gray and hazy domain of "victimless crimes"—in other words, no one is involved and no one is harmed except "consenting" adults. The organization maintains—in both its literature[18] and in the innumerable court cases it has undertaken[19]—that such crimes should fall entirely outside the concern of the community or the citizenry. It argues that to impose "community standards" of ethics and decency is "a violation of the spirit of American democracy"[20] and a "contradiction of our most basic constitutional tenants."[21] Any attempt to do so is instantly dubbed as "bigotry,"[22] or "zealotry and insensitivity,"[23] or "the excesses of religious fundamentalism."[24] You simply "can't legislate morality" says the organization.[25]

Legislating Morality

On the contrary, as Dr. D. James Kennedy has so often asserted, "Morality is the only thing you *can* legislate."[26] That's what legislation *is*. It is the codification in law of some particular moral concern – generally so that the immorality of a few is not forcibly inflicted on the rest of us.

Murder is against the law because we recognize that the premeditated killing of another human being is a violation of a very basic and fundamental moral principle – a moral principle that we all hold dear: the sanctity of human life. Theft is against the law because we recognize that taking someone else's belongings without permission is a breach of another one of our most basic and fundamental ethical standards: the inviolability of private property. The fact is, *all* law is some moral or ethical tenant raised up to social enforceability by the civil sphere.

Thus, the question is not "*Should* we legislate morality?" Rather, it is "*Whose* morality should we legislate?" The question is, "*What* moral standard will we use when we legislate?"

There was no ambivalence among founders of this nation on that question. The standard of morality that they unhesitatingly codified into law was the Bible. *The Declaration of Independence* was a document carefully informed by a Scriptural notion of law.[27] *The Articles of Confederation* were thoroughly entrenched in the Biblical worldview.[28] *The Constitution* was undeniably a Christian legal document.[29] *The Federalist Papers* were birthed of the great verities and profundities of liberty found only in the Bible.[30] *The Bill of Rights* would have been inconceivable apart from the moral standard wrought by God in His Word.[31] Every major document, every major consultation, and every major institution that the founding fathers forged from the fires of freedom to create and guide our remarkable legal system was a conscious affirmation and imitation of Biblical ideals, values, standards, ethics, and morals.

Now to be sure there were a number of other historical and philosophical influences that helped to shape the course of American law: Justinian's *Roman Civil Law*, Alfred the Great's *English Common Law*, Charlemagne's *Rule of the Franks*, William Blackstone's *Commentaries*, and John Locke's *Second Treatise on Civil Government*. However, each of these in turn were themselves derived, at least in part, from the Biblical standard.[32]

Robert Goguet, in his authoritative history of the development of judicial philosophy in this country, argued that the founding fathers' legislation of Biblical morality was more than simply a reflection of their personal faith or cultural inheritance, it was a matter of sober-headed practicality:

> The more they meditated on the Biblical standards for civil morality, the more they perceived their wisdom and inspiration. Those standards alone have the inestimable advantage never to have undergone any of the revolutions common to all human laws, which have always demanded frequent amendments; sometimes changes; sometimes additions; sometimes the retrenching of superfluities. There has been nothing changed, nothing added, nothing retrenched from Biblical morality for above three thousand years.[33]

The framers were heavily influenced by the writings of Thomas Hooker, founder of the City of Hartford in the Connecticut Colony and learned Puritan divine, and thus they agreed wholeheartedly with his oft quoted maxim on the wellspring of law and order in society:

> Of law there can be no less acknowledged, than that her seat is in the bosom of God, her voice in the harmony of the world. All things in heaven and on earth do her homage; the very least as doing her care, and the greatest as not exempt from her power. Both angels and men, and creatures of what condition soever, though each in a differ-

ent sort of name, yet all with one uniform consent, admire
her as the mother of their peace and joy.[34]

John Jay was one of the most influential of the founding
fathers and the first Chief Justice of the Supreme Court. He
too affirmed the necessity of virtue for the proper maintenance of civil stability and order:

> No human society has ever been able to maintain both
> order and freedom, both cohesiveness and liberty apart
> from the moral precepts of the Christian Religion applied
> and accepted by all the classes. Should our Republic ere
> forget this fundamental precept of governance, men are
> certain to shed their responsibilities for licentiousness and
> this great experiment will then surely be doomed.[35]

James Madison, our fourth President, primary author of
the Bill of Rights, and champion of liberty throughout the
founding era echoed that sentiment:

> We have staked the future of all our political institutions
> upon the capacity of each and all of us to govern ourselves,
> to control ourselves, and to sustain ourselves according to
> the Ten Commandments of God.[36]

Again and again that same refrain was repeated. The men
who framed our nation had a particular goal in mind: building a free society of responsible and morally upright men and
women. They wanted to build a "city on a hill," a "light to
the nations," and a godly legacy. They were willing to give
sacrificially—often giving their very lives and livelihoods—to
achieve those ends.

As a result, America became a *great* nation. It became
great because its character was rooted in Christian morality.
As Alexis de Toqueville asserted, "America is great because
America is good."[37]

Rights and Responsibilities

A brash and cavalier attitude to America's goodness and moral stalwartness is perhaps the single most distressing trait of the ACLU. In the name of civil liberties, it has pressed forward a radical agenda of moral corruption and ethical degeneration.

Ironically, its brazen disregard for decency and its passionately undeterred defense of perverse impropriety has actually *threatened* our liberties because it has threatened the *foundation* of those liberties.

The ACLU wants the privileges of America bestowed upon the citizenry as an unearned, undeserved, and unwarranted *entitlement.* Apart from the grace of God though, there simply can not be any such entitlement in human societies. Great privileges bring with them great responsibilities. Our remarkable freedom has been bought with a price. And that price was diligence, sacrifice, and moral uprightness. The legal commitment of the ACLU to the fanatically twisted fringe of American culture — pornographers, gay activists, abortionists, and other sexpert liberationists — is a pathetically self-defeating crusade that has confused liberty with license.

Gardiner Spring, the eloquent pastor-patriot during the early nineteenth century in New York, persuasively argued that the kind of free society America aspired to be was utterly and completely impossible apart from moral integrity:

> Every considerate friend of civil liberty, in order to be consistent with himself must be the friend of the Bible. No tyrant has ever effectually conquered and subjugated a people whose liberties and public virtue were founded upon the Word of God. After all, civil liberty is not freedom from restraint. Men may be wisely and benevolently checked, and yet be free. No man has a right to act as he thinks fit, irrespective of the wishes and interests of others. This would be exemption from all law, and from the wholesome influence of social institutions. Heaven itself would not be

free, if this were freedom. No created being holds any such liberty as this, by a divine warrant. The spirit of subordination, so far from being inconsistent with liberty, is inseparable from it.[38]

Similarly, Aleksandr Solzhenitsyn, the exiled Russian novelist, historian, and Nobel laureate, recently said:

Fifty years ago it would have seemed quite impossible in America that an individual be granted boundless freedom with no purpose but simply for the satisfaction of his whims. The defense of individual rights has reached such extremes as to make society as a whole defenseless. It is time to defend, not so much human rights, as human obligations.[39]

The ACLU desires to divorce rights from responsibilities. The danger is that if they ever do entirely succeed, rights will become extinct. "There is a way that seems right to a man, but its end is the way of death" (Proverbs 14:12).

Conclusion

The ACLU desperately wants to legislate morality. *Its* morality. Or should we say, its *immorality*. Despite all its high sounding rhetoric—limiting majorities to protect minorities— it is intent on remaking the American legal system after its own image.[40] It is intent on holding the majority captive to the fancies, follies, and foibles of the minority.

Freedom is a rare and delicate thing—as the last five thousand years of recorded human history readily attest. It can only survive in an ecology of Christian morality. Our founding fathers knew that only too well.

Therefore, if we genuinely desire Lady Liberty to kiss our land with her fresh fragrance and lush bounty, we had best turn from promiscuity and perversion, and fully embrace the values and virtues that our framers embraced: the values and virtues of the Bible.

It was the opinion of one of early America's most distinguished statesmen and jurists, Fisher Ames, that, "No man can be a sound lawyer in this land who is not well read in the ethics of Moses and the virtues of Jesus."[41]

That is as true today as it was then — regardless of what the ACLU may or may not believe.

8

CRIME AND PUNISHMENT

sine Christo, omnis virtus est in vito[1]

Private law has overcome public law.[2]

Hilaire Belloc

It is not true of course that crime is a disease. It is criminology that is a disease.[3]

G.K. Chesterton

Our nation is in the iron grip of a crime wave of epic proportions. But then, that is old news, isn't it? Sadly, it doesn't look to get better at any time in the foreseeable future. In fact, crime prognosticators are painting a very grim picture of the days ahead:

- According to the FBI's *Uniform Crime Reports*, the chance of being the victim of a major violent crime such as murder, rape, robbery, or aggravated assault nearly tripled during the two decades following 1960.[4] But then, it took only five more years to triple again.[5] And the risk continues to grow exponentially.

- Serious property crimes have increased even more rapidly. This year, one household out of every ten will be burglarized nationwide.[6]

- No one is safe. This year about twenty thousand murders will take place across our land.[7] In addition, nearly three-quarters of a million Americans will be injured in incidents of aggravated assault and other violent crimes.[8]

- No place is safe. Suburbs and small towns — the traditional havens from the hazards of urban crowding — have actually witnessed more dramatic increases in violent crime than have large cities.[9]

- The rapid increase in drug-related crime has put an ugly and vicious twist on growing up in this society. According to a recent Justice Department study, four out of every five American youngsters will become victims of malicious violence at one time or another.[10]

- That same study found that a shocking ninety-nine percent of Americans will be the victims of some serious crime at some time in their life.[11]

As Daniel Van Ness, president of Justice Fellowship, has asserted, "If you haven't already been a victim of crime, you will be. This is not a warning or a theory, it is a fact."[12]

Amazingly, a tiny segment of the population is responsible for the vast proportion of these crimes. So, even though the number of serious crimes committed in the United States over the past thirty years has increased nearly three hundred and fifty percent and arrests have risen more than two hundred and seventy percent,[13] the number of individuals involved in criminal activity has only increased about fifteen percent.[14] What that means in practical terms is that a remarkably small handful of brigands, thugs, and ruffians has been able to terrorize and paralyze our national life:

- Ninety percent of all the offenses listed in the FBI's *Crime Index* were perpetrated by multiple and repeat offenders.[15]

- Ninety-five percent of all robberies are attributable to that same cadre of hardened criminals.[16]

- Four out of five adults listed in the FBI's current *Criminal History File* are repeat offenders. They average just over five prior arrests apiece.[17]

- Despite this all too obvious pattern though, it is getting harder and harder to obtain criminal convictions. Three out of five arrests never come to trial. And six out of seven trials result in acquittals or releases due to technicalities.[18]

- Even in the instances when convictions can be obtained, inmates today serve less than half of their court-ordered sentences. On the average, they are back on the streets again in less than eighteen months.[19]

Though the ACLU claims to have the liberties and freedoms of all Americans at heart, its criminal justice positions, policies, and programs have only aggravated and exacerbated the already horrendous problems of maintaining law and order. Over the years it has waged innumerable court battles in order to:[20]

- Eliminate all prison sentencing from criminal judicial procedure except in a few "extreme" cases of utter incorrigibility — and only then as the penalty of last resort;

- Disallow capital punishment in any and all situations as a violation of the constitution's "cruel and unusual punishment" clause;

- Discredit deterrence as a basis for incarceration;

- Oppose rehabilitative confinement;

- Block all sentencing guidelines that seek restitution to the victims of criminal behavior;

- Mandate suspended sentences with probation as the primary form of "treatment" for criminal offenders;

- Restrict all court sentencing discretion through the legislative process or direct judicial intervention in trial proceedings — thus severely crippling the principle of trial by jury;

- Eliminate all mandatory sentencing laws;

- Facilitate mandatory early parole and release programs;

- And, oppose new construction or expansion of jails, prisons, and detention centers.

In addition to imposing these varied and various encumbrances to the operation of the correctional system in our land, the ACLU is also heavily involved in limiting the latitude and prerogatives of law enforcement agencies. Over the years it has sought to:[21]

- Severely restrict search and arrest procedures even when evidence of guilt is available;

- Hinder protective or corrective police action at crime scenes;

- Invalidate airport bomb detectors, drunk driving checkpoints, periodic or random drug screening, and other preventative security measures;

- Prohibit the free exchange of criminal records between law enforcement agencies;

- Limit even the most sound and non-prejudicial police interrogation and investigation techniques;

- Institute national or regional bureaucratic control over law enforcement agencies — thus effectively removing local accountability;

- Severely restrict riot control, swat team, and anti-terrorist activities and efforts;

- Make most surveillance operations, stakeout procedures, and community crackdowns illegal;

- Prohibit the eviction of drug dealers and other incorrigibles from public housing projects;

- Deregulate and decriminalize all "victimless crimes" — such as prostitution, drug use and abuse, gambling, sodomy, or the production, exhibition, and sale of vile and obscene materials — despite the proven link between such vices and serious crime;

- And, as if all that weren't bad enough, it has sought to impose strict gun control measures on both law enforcement agencies and on the citizenry at large, even to the point of banning firearms altogether — in spite of the Constitution's Second Amendment guarantee that the right "to keep and bear arms shall not be infringed."

The ACLU's approach to crime and punishment clearly reflects its historical roots in — and commitment to — revolutionary anarchism, radical socialism, and labor unrest. The organization has always been an unswerving adversary of law enforcement — distrusting its motives, scrutinizing its actions, and reveling in its weaknesses.[22] Thus, its perspective is colored almost entirely by a concern for the criminal element — leading some to charge that rather than being the defender of *civil* liberties, the ACLU is actually the champion of *criminal* liberties.[23] Roger Baldwin once actually admitted that he could not in good conscience serve on a jury because he simply "would never take part in convicting anyone."[24] When asked how our society could possibly continue to exist without some sort of penal justice system, he tersely snapped, "That's your problem."[25]

The Right to Do Right

"Is a society redeemed if it provides massive safeguards for accused persons," but fails to afford "elementary protection for its decent, law-abiding citizens," asked Supreme Court Chief Justice Warren Burger? Obviously not. That is why our founding fathers made certain that the primary focus of our criminal justice system would be victim's rights *not* criminal's rights.[26]

The delegates to Continental Congress, in documenting their grievances with King George's Parliament, asserted that the "certainty and lenity of the criminal law of England, and its benefits and advantages" had been effectually dissipated.[27] They argued that the system had over time been "subjected to arbitrary alterations," and had been reduced to "the precarious tenure of mere will."[28] As a result, freedom, justice, order, and true liberty were jeopardized. It was an intolerable situation and, they believed, a valid justification for their declaration of secession.[29]

In order to prevent that kind of deplorable situation from recurring in the new Republic, the founding fathers established a judicial system that was fair but tough, scrupulous but expeditious, objective but decisive, and circumspect but forthright. Mirroring the case law code of the Bible (Exodus 21–23), it was a system that focused first and foremost on the concerns of innocent and productive citizens: providing protection for them, establishing security for them, maintaining the common good for them, and making restitution to them. Only secondarily did it give careful scrutiny to the concerns of criminals: securing them against discrimination, affording them a fair and speedy trial before a jury of their peers, and guaranteeing them swift but humane punishment.

In other words, it was a system rooted in certain "inalienable rights." But, it was a system in which those rights were designed to give men *the right to do right*, not *the right to do wrong*. It was a system that made a clear ethical differentiation between liberty and license. As Gardiner Spring argued at the end of that remarkable founding era:

> Life, liberty, and property, peace, order, and public morals have not been left by the benevolent authors of our system of social existence and justice to chance, or anarchy, or the changing fashions of a social compact. Good is protected. Wickedness is penalized. Right is upheld above rights, for rights can only have meaning in the context of right. In any other context they are but perverse wranglings of prejudice, greed, and personal aggrandizement.[30]

Nathaniel Niles, the founding era's renowned and influential eleven-term congressman, state supreme court judge, farmer, and businessman from Vermont, reiterated this emphasis on victim's rights:

> There must be an exact proportion between an offense and its penalty. Where there is no such proportion, or equality, liberty is infringed, because the law is partial, as it will injure the public by not giving its due. . . . Justice must give first consideration to the good citizens of the community. No virtue can be inculcated when it pays first heed to the violent disrupters of the order.[31]

It was the unanimous opinion of the designers of the American penal system that the magistrates and the courts were to be the "stewards of the justice and virtue of heaven."[32] As a result, such Biblical approaches to upholding victim's rights as restitution (see Exodus 21:18–19), reparation (see Exodus 22:1–15), and community service (see Exodus 23:1–13) were added to incarceration, corporal punishment, and capital punishment — even to the point of dominating the American judicial ecology.[33] The focus of justice was not fixed on the criminal and his sundry vices but on the community and its welfare.[34]

Bewitched, Bothered, and Bewildered

The ACLU has managed to bury this remarkable legacy under the dust heap of litigation and adjudication. It has succeeded in practically reversing the emphasis of American justice — so that now it seems that criminals have more rights than law abiding citizens do. It has, in fact, conjured up a whole new system that according to Chuck Colson, often punishes "victims and taxpayers far more than offenders."[35] It is a "system on the brink of incoherence," argues Daniel Van Ness.[36] Rife with "inefficiency, low morale, prison overcrowding, revolving door release, and indifference at every turn," he says that it is a system that has quickly become "a joke to criminals, a mystery to victims, and a scandal to taxpayers."[37] The result is that, as the liberal columnist Carl Rowan has said, "We have all become hostages to crime and to the criminal justice system."[38] We have become a nation "bewitched, bothered, and bewildered" by the most complex and pernicious of forces.

For this desperate situation, we have the diligent efforts of the American Civil Liberties Union to thank.

The ACLU has made it a veritable vocation to be on the wrong side of the law. Even apart from its gleeful advocacy of criminal vices in our communities — the legalization of drugs, of prostitution, of hard core pornography, of aberrant sexual behavior, and of perverse solicitation — the organization is forever coddling and pampering criminal offenders with special legal privileges and initiatives while hampering and denigrating enforcement officials with bureaucratic red tape and stalling maneuvers. And all this at the taxpayer's expense. All this in the name of liberty.

Conclusion

According to Daniel Van Ness both the Biblical and the original American systems of justice demand at least four elements: securing public order, holding offenders accountable, ensuring repayment of victims, and restoration of community peace.[39] These are the virtues that must be upheld if our civil liberties are to be protected.

And yet, these are the very virtues that the ACLU is adamantly opposed to. So, far from insuring that our civil liberties are protected, the organization has for all intents and purposes become an advocacy group for organized crime, for teenage street gangs, for pornographers, for corrupt lawyers, and for illicit drug dealers. As a result, our civil liberties are actually imperiled.

In 1710, Cotton Mather, the great colonial mastermind, wrote a marvelous series of essays entitled *To Do Good*. His prophetic tenor is difficult to ignore, especially in light of the ACLU's agenda:

> How much hurt may be done by one wicked man or institution. Yea, sometimes one wicked man, of but small abilities, may do an incredible amount of mischief in the world by simply taking the opposite side of sense and truth. We will surely see, in the days not too far hence, some wretched instrument ply the intention of preserving liberty at a strange rate, until he has undone the entire country. It is a melancholy consideration, and I may say an astonishing one. In that day, you will hardly find one of a thousand, who does near so much to serve Christ as you may see done by thousands to serve the devil. A horrible thing.[40]

PART FOUR

THE STRATEGY

Whatever is buried right into our blood from the immemorial habit of holy tradition, we must be certain to do if we are to be fairly happy, and what is more important, decent and secure of our souls.[1]

Hilaire Belloc

The homeless skepticism of our time has reached a sub-conscious feeling that morality is somehow a matter of human taste — an accident of psychology.[2]

G.K. Chesterton

9

WHAT THE WORLD NEEDS NOW
curae morborum[3]

There is a complex knot of forces underlying any nation once Christian; a smoldering of the old fires.[4]

Hilaire Belloc

The modern world is full of the old Christian virtues gone mad. The virtues have gone mad because they have been isolated from each other and are wandering alone. Thus some scientists care for truth; but their truth is pitiless. And thus, some humanitarians only care for pity; but their pity — I am sorry to say — is often untruthful.[5]

G.K. Chesterton

On October 27, 1787, Alexander Hamilton predicted that a "dangerous ambition" would one day tyrannize the gangling young American Republic, all the while lurking "behind the specious mask of zeal for the *rights* of the people."[6]

It could almost be said that Hamilton had the ACLU in mind when he wrote that — despite the fact that it would not be founded for another century. Certainly, the organization legitimately falls under the purview of his warning. It has exercised its "dangerous ambition" all across our land in classrooms, courtrooms, and communities, wreaking havoc on our families, our neighborhoods, our schools, our businesses, and our system of justice. And it has done this, all the while lurking behind the "specious mask" that Hamilton described so long ago. It has done this, all the while zealously championing "the *rights* of the people."

What the ACLU has done, though — as awful and tyrannical as it has been — is not nearly as disconcerting as *what the ACLU is.* Its actions and activities are merely symptoms of a deeper, darker cancer. They are merely the *outward expressions* of its "dangerous ambition."

That "ambition" is actually a worldview.

The word *worldview* is actually a poor English attempt at translating the German *weltanschauung.* It literally means *a philosophical orientation, a life perspective,* or *a life integrator.*

You have a worldview. I have a worldview. Everyone does.

Our worldview is simply the way we look at things. It is our perspective of reality. It is the means by which we interpret the situations and circumstances around us. It is what enables us to integrate all the different aspects of our life, faith, and experience. Alvin Toffler, in his landmark book *Future Shock,* said, "Every person carries in his head a mental model of the world, a subjective representation of external reality."[7] This mental model is, he says, like a giant filing cabinet. It contains a slot for every item of information coming to us. It organizes our knowledge and gives us a grid from which to think. Our mind is not as Voltaire would have us suppose: a *tabla rasa,* blank and impartial. Our viewpoint is not open and objective. "When we think," says economic philosopher E.F. Schumacher, "we can only do so because our mind is already filled with all sorts of ideas with which to think."[8] These more or less fixed ideas make up our mental model of the world, our frame of reference, our presuppositions — or, in other words, our worldview.

James Sire tells us:

> A worldview is a map of reality; and like any map, it may
> fit what is really there, or it may be grossly misleading. The
> map is not the world itself, of course, only an image of it,
> more or less accurate in some places, distorted in others.
> Still, all of us carry around such a map in our mental
> makeup and we act upon it. All of our thinking presup-
> poses it. Most of our experience fits into it.[9]

Throughout the history of mankind, there have been any
number of worldviews espoused by ardent and articulate partisans. But, there is one particular worldview that has become
only too familiar to us—actually dominating our cultural apparatus—in these modern times. That worldview and the ad-
herents that extol its virtues have been brilliantly described
by the twentieth century's foremost historian, Paul Johnson:

> With the decline of clerical power in the eighteenth cen-
> tury, a new kind of mentor emerged to fill the vacuum and
> capture the ear of society. The secular intellectual might be
> deist, skeptic, or atheist. But he was just as ready as any
> pontiff or presbyter to tell mankind how to conduct its af-
> fairs. He proclaimed from the start, a special devotion to
> the interests of humanity and an evangelical duty to ad-
> vance them by his teaching. He brought to this self-ap-
> pointed task a far more radical approach than his clerical
> predecessors. He felt himself bound by no corpus of re-
> vealed religion. The collective wisdom of the past, the leg-
> acy of tradition, the prescriptive codes of ancestral experi-
> ence existed to be selectively followed or wholly rejected
> entirely as his own good sense might decide. For the first
> time in human history, and with growing confidence and
> audacity, men arose to assert that they could diagnose the
> ills of society and cure them with their own unaided intel-
> lects: more, that they could devise formulae whereby not
> merely the structure of society but the fundamental habits
> of human beings could be transformed for the better. Un-

like their sacerdotal predecessors, they were not servants and interpreters of the gods but substitutes. Their hero was Prometheus, who stole the celestial fire and brought it to earth.[10]

The worldview that Johnson is describing is what has recently come to be called *secular humanism*. It is the worldview that the "dangerous ambition" of the ACLU epitomizes and espouses.

According to Francis Schaeffer, secular humanism is "the placing of man at the center of all things and making him the measure of all things."[11] According to Aleksandr Solzhenitsyn, it is, "the proclaimed and practiced autonomy of man from any higher force above him."[12] In the humanistic system, there is no ultimate standard of right or wrong. There are no clear cut ethical paradigms. Morality is relative. Problem solving is entirely subjective. Paradoxically then, the only absolute is that there are no absolutes.

In direct contradistinction to humanism—serving as its chief adversary—is the Christian worldview. According to this system, there are indeed standards, paradigms, and absolutes (see Exodus 20:3–17). They are to be found in the Bible (see Deuteronomy 6:4–19). And they are to be found *only* in the Bible (see 1 Corinthians 4:6). This is because only the Bible can tell us of things as they *really* are (see Psalm 19:7–11). Only the Bible enables us to face reality squarely, practically, completely, and honestly (see Deuteronomy 30:11–14). Thus, only the Bible can provide us with genuine solutions to the problems that have always plagued mankind (see Psalm 119:105).

Jesus constantly reminded His followers of these facts. He made it clear that the Bible was to be their only rule— for life and godliness, for faith and practice, for profession and confession:

It is written, "Man shall not live by bread alone, but by every word that proceeds from the mouth of God." (Matthew 4:4)

It is easier for heaven and earth to pass away than for one tittle of the Law to fail. (Luke 16:17)

Whoever therefore breaks one of the least of these Commandments, and teaches men so, shall be called least in the kingdom of heaven; but whoever does and teaches them, he shall be called great in the kingdom of heaven. (Matthew 5:19)

And it was not merely Jesus who emphasized this. It is a constant theme throughout all of revelation:

The law of the LORD is perfect, converting the soul; the testimony of the LORD is sure, making wise the simple. The statutes of the LORD are right, rejoicing the heart; the commandment of the LORD is pure, enlightening the eyes. The fear of the LORD is clean, enduring forever; the judgments of the LORD are true and righteous altogether. More to be desired are they than gold, yea, than much fine gold; sweeter also than honey and the honey comb. Moreover, by them Your servant is warned; and in keeping them there is great reward. (Psalm 19:7–11)

Your Word is a lamp to my feet, and a light to my path. I have sworn and confirmed that I will keep Your righteous judgements. (Psalm 119:105–106)

All Scripture is given by inspiration of God and is profitable for doctrine, for reproof, for correction, for instruction in righteousness, that the man of God may be complete, thoroughly equipped for every good work. (2 Timothy 3:16–17)

We also have the prophetic Word made more sure, which you do well to heed as a light that shines in a dark place,

until the day dawns and the morning star rises in your
hearts; knowing this first, that no prophesy of Scripture is
of any private interpretation, for prophesy never came by
the will of man, but holy men of God spoke as they were
moved by the Holy Spirit. (2 Peter 1:19–21)

All those who have gone on before us in faith, laying the
foundations of freedom that we now enjoy—forefathers, fathers, patriarchs, prophets, apostles, preachers, evangelists,
martyrs, confessors, ascetics, and every righteous spirit made
pure in Christ—have had this perspective as the foundation
and frame of their worldview.

They understood that to attempt to solve the perilous
problems of human society without hearing and heeding the
clear instructions of the Bible is utter foolishness (see Romans
1:18–23). It is to be out of sync with reality (see Isaiah 8:20).
It is to invite inadequacy, incompetence, and failure (see
Deuteronomy 28:15).

The lawyers, political activists, and social reformers in the
ACLU certainly cannot be faulted for their concern for the
rights of people—to the extent that they really are concerned
about those rights. Where they have gone wrong—and ultimately what makes their "ambition" so "dangerous"—is in
taking matters into their own hands. It is in stealing the "celestial fire." It is in canonizing their own new and novel notions—of law, morality, social relations, and whatever else.
Instead of adhering to the wise and inerrant counsel of Scripture—walking along the well-trod path of the saints—they
have "turned, every one, to his own way" (Isaiah 53:6), and
done "what was right in his own eyes" (Judges 21:25).

Two Covenants

The philosophical, ethical, and cultural foundation for
worldviews—whether Christian or humanistic—is *covenantal.*
The Bible defines the idea of covenant as the personal, bind-

ing, and structural relationship between the various component parts of any given society. It is the means by which we
approach, deal with, and know one another—and God. It is
the pattern of all our relationships. It is the divine-to-human
and human-to-divine and human-to-human social structure.

Thus, covenantalism is woven into the fabric of man's very
being. It is an inescapable reality. It gives shape to all our thinking and all our doing—whether we actually know it or not. Our
worldview is, therefore, necessarily covenantal in nature.

The Biblical covenant has at least five basic component
parts.[13] It begins with the establishment of God's nature and
character: He is sovereign. Next, it proclaims God's authority:
He has established order and structure. Third, the covenant
outlines God's stipulations: He has given His people responsibilities. Fourth, it establishes God's judicial see: He will one
day sit in judgment. And finally, the covenant details God's
very great and precious promises: He has laid up an inheritance for the faithful.

This outline of the covenant, though by no means absolute, can be seen, in at least an oblique fashion, in God's
dealings with Adam (see Genesis 1:26–31; 2:16–25), Noah
(see Genesis 9:1–17), Abraham (see Genesis 12:1–3; 15:1–
21), Moses (see Exodus 3:1–22), and the disciples of Christ
(see 1 Corinthians 11:23–34). It is also evident in some way,
shape, form, or another in the Ten Commandments (two ta-
bles of five statutes), the structure of the Pentateuch (five
books), the book of Deuteronomy (five parts), the book of
Psalms (five sections), the book of Revelation (five stages),
and many other passages of Scripture in both the Old and
New Testaments.

As a result, the Christian worldview—derived as it is from
the teaching of Scripture—revolves around and is defined in
terms of the Biblical covenant: the Sovereignty of God, the
structure of His order, the pattern of His ethics, the reality of
His judgment, and the hope of His promise.

Because all worldviews are covenantal at their root, it is not surprising to discover that the humanistic worldview can also be capsulized and summarized in five primary and primordial presuppositions: secularism, egalitarianism, rationalism, anti-traditionalism, and optimism. These are the five "values, beliefs, and sentiments" that Heritage Foundation scholar, William Donohue, says are constitutive of modern humanism.[14] And they are, he says, the values, beliefs, and sentiments "through which the ACLU sees the world," as well.[15]

Side by side, the two covenants—the Christian and the humanistic—as well as their corresponding worldviews, make for a very interesting contrast (see table 9.1):

Table 9.1 Covenants	
The Christian Covenant	*The Humanistic Covenant*
God's sovereignty	Man-centered secularism
God's order	Man-imposed egalitarianism
God's ethics	Man-generated rationalism
God's judgment	Man-induced anti-traditionalism
God's promises	Man-provoked optimism

Obviously, each of these covenants produces dramatically different worldviews. And just as obviously, each of these worldviews produces dramatically different societies.

That anthropological, sociological, and theological fact was borne out in a very vivid fashion during the late eighteenth century during the tumultuous aftermath of the American and French Revolutions.

Two Revolutions

The revolutionary era ushered in an ethos of convulsing paradox and enrapturing cataclysm that was captured in the opening scene of *A Tale of Two Cities*, the riveting novel by Charles Dickens:

> It was the best of times, it was the worst of times, it was the age of wisdom, it was the age of foolishness, it was the epoch of belief, it was the epoch of incredulity, it was the season of Light, it was the season of Darkness, it was the spring of hope, it was the winter of despair, we had every thing before us, we had nothing before us, we were all going directly to Heaven, we were all going direct the other way.[16]

The passage concludes saying:

> In short, the period was so far like the present period, that some of its noisiest authorities insisted on its being received, for good or for evil, in the superlative degree of comparison only.[17]

The dichotomous nature of the era that Dickens first describes and then applies, was surely the result of the dichotomous relationship of its two great events: the American Revolution of 1776 and the French Revolution of 1789.

Two more widely polarized yet interdependent events cannot possibly be dredged from the tattered annals of western civilization. Though, by all appearances, they were like *dideros* and *videros* — practically identical in seed, root, sprig, blossom, and fruit — they were in fact, as different as *chalmedia* and *tralmedia* — entirely unrelated genuses.[18] Indeed, as Stephen Higginson has asserted, the two revolutions actually "drew a red-hot ploughshare through history."[19]

According to the prominent American historian Garry Wills:

There were two great revolutions against European monarchs in the late eighteenth century. In the first, the French nation helped Americans achieve their independence from George III. Without that help, our revolution could not have succeeded. Yet when the French rebelled against Louis XVI, Americans at first merely hailed their action, then hesitated over it, and finally recoiled from it.[20]

Why was that? Why did the founding fathers of the newly independent American republic reject their brothers-in-arms from across the Atlantic? Why did they not rally to the Jacobin cry of "Liberty, Equality, and Fraternity?" Why did they not rush to the aid of the embattled masses of France struggling to be free of a monarchical tyrant?

The answer is simple: worldview. The American leaders recognized that the worldview of the French Jacobins was rooted in the humanistic covenant and was thus entirely incompatible with their own — that it was in fact, detrimental to their own.

The American revolution was a covenantal Christian response to what was perceived to be a graceless trouncing of the rule of law. It gave rise to an extraordinary and unparalleled reign of freedom, peace, and prosperity. It was a *conservative* movement in the sense of *returning* the estate of the nation to the *old* virtues of Christian civilization.[21] The former royal colonists understood the term *revolution* in the Copernican sense of *coming full circle, to revolve,* or *to return to an original state.* Thus, they conducted themselves with the utmost in decorum and ethics.

The French Revolution, on the other hand, was a covenantally deliberate affront to Christianity. It gave rise to a horrifying reign of anarchy and terror that cost the lives of tens of thousands of innocent citizens and burned itself out in brazen licentiousness and concupiscence. It was a *liberal* movement in the sense of *dispatching* the estate of the nation from the *old* virtues of Christendom while ushering the *new* amoralities of the Enlightenment.[22] The former royal subjects understood the term *revolution* in the Rousseauian sense of *starting anew, to revolt*, or *to overthrow a former state.* Thus, they conducted themselves with the height of perversion and violence.

Rhetorically and theoretically, both revolutions made much over the ideals of liberty, freedom, and justice. But, whereas the American effort had scattered seeds of faithfulness, forthrightness, fealty, and fulfillment to the four corners of the earth, the French effort had sown seeds of doubt, dissension, discord, and devastation to the four winds. The American revolution was a "lofty aspiration" exercised. The French revolution was a "dangerous ambition" exorcised.

It was with this understanding as a backdrop that Alexander Hamilton decried the French disruptions in a letter to his friend, the Marquis de Lafayette, saying:

> When I contemplate the horrid and systematic massacres of the Jacobins; when I observe that a Marat and a Robespierre, the notorious promoters of those bloody scenes, sit triumphantly in the convention and take a conspicuous part in its measures, that an attempt to bring the assassins to justice has been obliged to be abandoned; when I see an unfortunate prince, whose reign was a continued demonstration of the goodness and benevolence of his heart, his attachment to the people of whom he was the monarch, who though educated in the lap of despotism, had given repeated proofs that *he was not the enemy of liberty,* brought precipitately and ignominiously to the block without any substantial proof of guilt as yet disclosed — without even an authentic exhibition of motives in decent regard to the opinions of mankind; *when I find the doctrines of Atheism openly advanced in the convention and heard with loud applause;* when I see the sword of *fanaticism* extended to force a political creed upon citizens who were invited to submit to the arms of France as the harbingers of liberty; when I behold *the hand of rapacity* outstretched to prostrate and ravish the monuments of religious worship erected by

those citizens and their ancestors; when I perceive passion, tumult, and violence usurping those seats where reason and cool deliberation ought to prevail, I acknowledge that I am glad to believe *there is no real resemblance between what was the cause of America and what is the cause of France; that the difference is no less great than the difference between liberty and licentiousness.* I regret whatever has the tendency to compound them, and I feel anxious as an American, that the ebullitions of inconsiderate men among us may not tend to involve our reputation in the issue.[23]

Hamilton understood that the worldview of the French revolutionaries would inevitably lead them — and all those around them — into a quagmire of death and destruction regardless of their slogans or intentions. He knew that true and lasting liberty is simply not possible apart from the gracious environs of the Christian worldview. And any attempt to so achieve it, is doomed. It is a "dangerous ambition." In fact, he ominously predicted that: "After wading through seas of blood, France may find herself at length the slave of some victorious Sulla or Marius or Caesar."[24]

Within six years of that prophesy, Napoleon had indeed usurped the authority of the republican leadership — or what was left of it after more than a decade of utter chaos. France was then plunged into the darkest chapter in its long history, and Europe began its long and tortured struggle with one tyrant after another.

Hamilton was no seer. He simply comprehended the impact and end result of the revolution's presuppositions. He was perceptive enough to look past its first appearances to consider its root. He knew that cosmetic adjustments in France's policies or programs would not make any substantial difference in the nation's ultimate destiny. He recognized that for life, liberty, and the pursuit of happiness to be restored to France, the humanistic worldview would have to be uprooted and replaced — and the Christian worldview would have to be reconfirmed in the cultural apparatus. More importantly though, he realized that in order for America to maintain its own liberty, the "dangerous ambition" of humanism had to be kept out of our social institutions.

The Apostle James paints the picture for us in hues of stark reality:

Does a spring send forth fresh water and bitter from the same opening? Can a fig tree, my brethren, bear olives, or a grapevine produce figs? Thus no spring can yield both salt water and fresh. (James 3:11–12)

Likewise, liberty and license cannot spring from the same source. A Christian worldview unequally yoked to a humanistic worldview is an impossible pluralism. In order for the ACLU to achieve its ends, the Christian foundations of our nation would have to be sundered. And by the same token, in order for those Christian foundations to be protected from the ACLU, the covenantal perspective of the Christian worldview will necessarily have to be nurtured, inculcated, and established in our own lives and in the culture at large.

"Where the Spirit of the Lord is," the Apostle Paul tells us, "there is liberty" (2 Corinthians 3:17). But where He is not, it is not.

The Totality of Life

Jesus is Lord. He is Lord over the totality of life. One of the basic demands of Christian discipleship is to *change* our way of thinking — about *everything*. We are to "bring every thought into captivity to the obedience of Christ" (2 Corinthians 10:5). We are not to "be conformed to this world but be transformed by the renewing of [our] minds" (Romans 12:2). In other words, we are commanded to have a Christian worldview. All our thinking, our perspective on life, and our understanding of the world around us—the totality of our life—is to be comprehensively informed by Scripture.

God's condemnation of the people of ancient Israel came because their ways were not His ways, and their thoughts were not His thoughts (see Isaiah 55:8). They did not have a consistent Scriptural worldview. When we begin to think about law or justice or rights or liberty or anything else apart from God's revelation, we open ourselves up to the same charge. We make ourselves vulnerable to the same condemnation. A Christian worldview is not optional. It is mandatory.

How do we go about developing such a worldview? How do we go about replacing our old ways of thinking with God's way of thinking?

Obviously, the place to start is with the Bible itself. We need to read the Bible with new eyes of awareness and alertness. We need to come to it with a new hunger for comprehensive truth. We need to familiarize ourselves with its full contents and with its whole counsel. Everything that we do, everything that we are about, all that we aspire to, and all that we pass on in legacy to the next generation, ought to be shaped by the clear teaching of Scripture. The Bible should be a virtual blueprint for every area of life—the totality of life. The revelation of God to man in the Bible is the authoritative starting point and the final court of appeal on earth. With confidence, we can approach every practical and theoretical discipline on the assumption that all forms of knowledge not rooted in the Christian worldview have been constructed on foundations of philosophical, moral, and spiritual sand. Thus, we can say with the prominent reformed theologian of the last generation, Cornelius Van Til, that, "The Bible is authoritative on everything of which it speaks. And it speaks of everything."[25]

We must hammer out principles of social reform in terms of God's Word. We must develop political perspectives based upon God's commands. We must construct standards of justice derived from God's precepts. And, we must pioneer ethics, morals, and values that are Scripturally grounded. Everything in every field, on every front, must be built on a fundamental rejection of the notion that there might be areas of intellectual, cultural, or spiritual neutrality. Every realm of human endeavor must flow from Biblical principles—because God has ordained that the Bible govern them all.

We cannot expect to create a utopian ideal, of course. Nor can we expect to be entirely consistent in our application of Biblical truth. Far from it. As mere fallen men and women, we will, like our fathers and forefathers before us make mistakes. Often. Even so, we must be insistent on obeying Scripture to the best of our ability across the board. And, with our belief in the comprehensiveness of the Bible's message, and our unwavering trust in the promises of God, we can be assured that God will covenantally bless us with success, just as He blessed them (see Deuteronomy 28:1–14).

It is not enough for us to simply *oppose* the ACLU's policies and programs of inhuman humanism. If we are to restore sanity to the American legal system and return a goodly measure of liberty to our cultural apparatus, then we must *propose* a positive alternative rooted in the Christian worldview.

This is the point that Jesus was trying to impress upon His disciples saying:

> When an unclean spirit goes out of a man, he goes through dry places, seeking rest, and finds none. Then he says, "I will return to my house from which I came." And when he comes, he finds it empty, swept, and put in order. Then he goes, and takes with him seven other spirits more wicked than himself, and they enter and dwell there; and the last state of that man is worse than the first. So shall it also be with this wicked generation. (Matthew 12:43–45)

We can't fight something with nothing. We can't *just say no* to the permutations of the ACLU. We can't simply clean house.

Thus, even though we need to begin to develop counterstrategies to meet the likes of the ACLU in the courts, in the media, in our schools, and in our local communities, we've got to make certain that we don't put the cart before the horse. We've got to make absolutely certain that we have a fully orbed worldview that yields to the Lordship of Christ in the totality of life.

Conclusion

Ideas have consequences.[26] Worldviews make a difference.[27] Covenants alter the course of cultures — and ultimately of all of history.[28] To fail to realize this basic and fundamental truth is to miss the import of social relations in space and time altogether.

The ACLU advocates a particular worldview. It is the same worldview that brought disaster upon the French during the dire days of the revolution two hundred years ago. It is the worldview of humanism — the covenantal opposite of Christianity.

If we are ever to turn the tide of immorality and illegality back, then we must not simply lodge our complaint against the ACLU's minions. Instead, we must begin to establish in our lives, our families, our churches, and our communities in a comprehensive Christian worldview.

In January of 1776, George Wythe of Virginia asked John Adams to draw up a plan that would enable the American colonies to establish a constitutional system strong enough to survive the rigors of war with England and to meet the challenges of the months and years following that. Adams replied with his usual discernment, discretion, and wisdom:

> The foundation of every nation is some principle or passion in the minds of the people. The noblest principles and most generous affections in our Christian character, then, have the fairest chance to support the noblest and the most generous models of civil covenant. If liberty and justice for all men is to be ensured then we cannot, we dare not, we must not stray from the Writ of right.[29]

10

REPAIRERS OF THE BREACH

acta sanctorum[1]

One should never leave a man without giving him something to show, by way of token, on the Day of Judgment.[2]

Hilaire Belloc

Despotism can be a development, often a late development and very often indeed the end of societies that have been highly democratic. A despotism may almost be defined as a tired democracy. As fatigue falls on a community, the citizens are less inclined for that eternal vigilance which has truly been called the price of liberty.[3]

G.K. Chesterton

I n 1917, when American troops were preparing to sail across the seas to take to the battlefields of France and Belgium in the First World War, the New York Bible Society asked former President Theodore Roosevelt to inscribe a message in the pocket New Testaments that each soldier would be given. The great man happily complied, writing:

The teaching of the New Testament is foreshadowed in Micah's verse: "What more doth the Lord require of thee than to *do justice,* and to *love mercy,* and to *walk humbly* with thy God." *Do justice;* and therefore fight valiantly against those that stand for the reign of Moloch and Beelzebub on this earth. *Love mercy;* treat your enemies well; succor the afflicted; treat every woman as if she were your sister; care for the little children; and be tender with the old and helpless. *Walk humbly;* you will do so if you study the life and teachings of the Savior, walking in His steps. And remember: the most perfect machinery of government will not keep us as a nation from destruction if there is not within us a soul. No abounding of material prosperity shall avail us if our spiritual senses atrophy. The foes of our own household will surely prevail against us unless there be in our people an inner life which finds its outward expression in a morality like unto that preached by the seers and prophets of God when the grandeur that was Greece and the glory that was Rome still lay in the future.[4]

Roosevelt understood only too well the essence of Biblical ethics and public policy. He understood that the security of men and nations depends on a faithful adherence to Micah's threefold demonstration of discipleship: a strident commitment to the just application of law (see Romans 2:11–24; James 2:8–13), a practical concern for the unfortunate (see James 1:27; Philippians 2:4), and a reverent fear of Almighty God (see Acts 10:34–35; Proverbs 1:7). He knew that even with the deployment of superior forces in superior numbers with superior armaments, the American armies would ultimately be defeated during the war if they took to the field bereft of these essential spiritual resources.

Similarly, if we are to be successful in developing Biblical strategies that can effectively counter the legal and cultural agenda of the ACLU, then we too must nurture a keen submission to the principled disciplines of justice, mercy, and humility before God.

Justice

Throughout the Bible the attributes of justice and righteousness are inextricably linked. In more than sixty different passages all across the wide span of the Old and New Testaments, God's Word makes it plain that to attempt to secure life, liberty, and the pursuit of happiness apart from the clearly revealed ethical parameters of goodness, truth, purity, faithfulness, and holiness is utter folly. On the other hand, a people that diligently seeks to do right—to do righteousness—will inevitably pursue justice as well. The two simply go together. One cannot be had without the other.

Again and again the refrain sounds: "Thus says the LORD: Keep justice and do righteousness, for my salvation is about to come, and my righteousness to be revealed" (Isaiah 56:1). "[The LORD] loves righteousness and justice" (Psalm 33:5). "Righteousness and justice are the foundation of Your [the LORD's] throne. Mercy and truth go before Your face" (Psalm 89:14). "He will bring forth justice for truth" (Isaiah 42:3). "[The LORD] says: 'I will make justice the measuring line and righteousness the plummet'" (Isaiah 28:17). "Blessed are those who keep justice, And he who does righteousness at all times" (Psalm 106:3). "Learn to do good; Seek justice" (Isaiah 1:17). "Hate evil, love good, and establish justice in the gate. It may be that the LORD God of hosts will be gracious" (Amos 5:15). "But let justice run down like a water, And righteousness like a mighty stream" (Amos 5:24).

Because Jesus emphasized this very unity between moral purity and juridical integrity in His earthly ministry, He continually found Himself in conflict with the religious leaders of His day—the Pharisees—as well as the secularists—the Herodians. Neither cared for His Biblically rooted insistence that justice was impossible apart from righteousness, and vice versa.

The Pharisees were a sect of religious fundamentalists. The Herodians were a sect of political statists. The Pharisees' name literally meant *the separatists*, concerned as they were with keeping themselves "unstained" by the world. The Herodians' name, on the other hand, implied a close connection with one of the most xenophobic and worldly men in all of history. The Pharisees withdrew from occupations of influence and justice in order to focus on "spiritual" things. The Herodians grasped for such occupations with undeterred zeal in order to focus on "earthly" things.

Yet, despite being so obviously poles apart in every way imaginable, these two sects were united in their opposition to Jesus (see Matthew 22:16; Mark 3:6; 12:13). Humanism makes for strange bedfellows: the Pharisaic sons of Jacob became the philosophical and practical accomplices of the Herodian sons of Esau (see Mark 3:8).

The Pharisees opposed Jesus because they felt He had "polluted" the spiritual realm with such "earthly" cares as protecting the innocent, succoring the sick, feeding the hungry, and nurturing the poor. The Herodians opposed Jesus because they felt He had "polluted" the earthly realm with such "spiritual" cares as preaching moral uprightness, proclaiming God's sovereignty over every sphere of life, and condemning hypocrisy wherever it may have been found. So, the two oddly matched sects—the pietistic escapists and the materialistic autonomists—became humanistic co-belligerents. They joined forces to assert and enforce an unholy separation between justice and righteousness.

Interestingly, after nearly two millennia, the two sects still exist. And they are still joined together in opposition to the message of Christ—which is *both* just and good.

The sect of the Pharisees is all too often represented by the church, of all things. We have, for all intents and purposes, abandoned our God-ordained duty to be salt and light in the midst of this poor fallen world (see Matthew 5:13–16). We have woefully neglected our cultural mandate (see Genesis 1:28) and our commission to disciple the nations (see Matthew 28:19–20). Instead, we have tended to emphasize a Pharisaic or separatist view of piety wherein a sharp division is made between the "spiritual" and the "earthly." Since we—like the Pharisees before us—often consider the "supernatural" realm to be somehow "superior" to the "natural," all things physical, all things temporal, and all things earthly are practically spurned. The arena of law and justice is thus left in the hand of evil doers. Although the Bible asserts that we are to think hard about the nature of Christian civilization (see 1 Peter 1:13), to try to develop Biblical alternatives to humanistic society (see Matthew 18:15–20), to prophesy Biblically to the cultural problems of our age (see Isaiah 6:8), and to pursue justice in tandem with our righteousness (see 1 Kings 10:9), we have isolated ourselves behind the walls of a vast evangelical ghetto. We have not only rendered unto Caesar what is Caesar's, we have rendered unto him what is God's as well. For the sake of righteousness we have neglected justice—and thus we have neither.

Meanwhile, the modern sect of the Herodians is busy with the work of oppression and repression. The Herodians hold the seats of power: in government, in law, in education, in the media, in medicine, and in the judiciary. They care nothing for our morality. They abhor our "puritanical" values. They chafe against our piety. They despise our non-conformity. *But, they applaud our irrelevancy.* They appreciate our distraction from the things of this earth. They know that as long as *we* separate righteousness and justice, *they* will continue to have free reign. They will be able to continue to reshape life, liberty, and the pursuit of happiness in their own image. They will be able to perpetuate their slaughter of the unborn, their assault on the family, their defamation of all things holy, all things sacred, and all things pure. They will be able to transfer deity and rule from God Almighty to themselves, doing what is right in their own eyes (see Judges 21:25).

The fact is though, they couldn't do what they do without us.

Gouverneur Morris, the great merchant, lawyer, and planter from Pennsylvania who actually drafted the final version of the Constitution, believed with John Adams, James Madison, George Washington, and the other framers that in order for the American experiment in liberty to succeed, justice and righteousness had to be "welded together as one in the hearts and minds of the citizenry."[5] He greatly feared the "fanatical ideology of the Jacobin French Republic,"[6] and yearned that America ever be steadfast in its "Christian consensus."[7] He said:

> Liberty and justice simply cannot be had apart from the gracious influences of a righteous people. A righteous people simply cannot exist apart from the aspiration to liberty and justice. The Christian religion and its incumbent morality is tied to the cause of freedom with a Gordian knot; loose one from the other and both are sent asunder.[8]

Clearly, if we are to be successful in developing Biblical strategies that can effectively counter the legal and cultural agenda of the ACLU, then we must recognize and reassert the connection between justice and righteousness. We must not only stand steadfast against any Herodian tendencies to remove morality from the arena of law, we must be equally vigilant in opposing any Pharisaical tendencies to remove justice from the arena of spirituality.

May we ever be able to say with Job, "I put on righteousness, and it clothed me; My justice was like a robe and a turban" (Job 29:14).

Mercy

Like justice and righteousness, mercy and authority are inseparable concepts according to the Biblical scheme of things. If we are ever to influence our culture to stand for truth, goodness, and justice, then we must graciously *serve* the hurts, wants, and needs all around us. Just as God has shown us mercy we must demonstrate mercy to others (see 2 Corinthians 1:3–7).

In 1929, the Council of Religious Affairs in the Soviet Union was instructed by Josef Stalin and the Central Committee of the Communist Party to enforce a comprehensive "ban on charitable or cultural activities by churches."[9] According to Vladimir Kharchev, a spokesman for the Kremlin at the time, "The State cannot tolerate any challenge to its claim on the heartstrings of the Russian people."[10]

Stalin, Kharchev, and the Soviet leadership understood only too well the connection between authority and merciful service. They understood the very Biblical notion that whoever becomes the "benefactor" of the people will ultimately be able to wield authority with them (see Luke 22:25).

This is one of the most basic principles of the Christian worldview: the ability to lead a society is earned not inherited. And it is earned through faithful, compassionate, and merciful service.

Unfortunately, this is not a principle that has been widely understood by the modern church—even by those of us actively involved in the public sector.

Servanthood—the ministry of exercising mercy—is a much neglected, largely forgotten Christian vocation today. It has been a coalition of humanists that has claimed the moral high ground by championing the causes of the hurting, the poor, and the outcast. It has been a motley band of bureaucrats, social reactionaries, and judicial activists that have won the hearts of the people—despite the impotence and inadequacy of their programs—because they have at least made a pretense of mercy.

What a terrible irony. Jesus made it plain that if the Christian community wants to have the authority to speak into the lives of the people around us, to give moral vision to our culture, and to ultimately shape civil justice we must not

grasp at the reins of power and prominence. We must serve.
We must live lives marked by mercy.

Money, manpower, and mailing lists — as fine and as important as those things may be — are not the keys to cultural
transformation. Mercy is.

Jesus was a servant (see Luke 22:27). He came to serve,
not to be served (see Matthew 20:20). He came offering
mercy at every turn (see Mark 5:19; Matthew 9:13).

Not surprisingly, He called His disciples to a similar life of
selfless giving (see Luke 22:26). He called us to be servants
(see Matthew 19:30). He said, "Whoever desires to be first
among you, let him be your slave" (Matthew 20:27). He said,
"Be merciful, just as your Father also is merciful" (Luke 6:36).
The attitude of all aspiring leaders should be the same as
Christ's, "who, being in the form of God, did not consider it
robbery to be equal with God, but made Himself of no reputation, taking the form of a servant" (Philippians 2:5–7).

If we are indeed going to influence our society with righteousness, truth, and justice we are going to have to learn the
lost art of servanthood. We are going to have to comprehend
the connection between mercy and authority.

The fact is, modern men are looking for proof. They want
evidence.

Genuine mercy is that evidence. It verifies the remarkable
claims of Scripture. It tells men that there is indeed a sovereign and gracious God who raises up a faithful people. It tells
men that God then blesses those people and gives them
workable solutions to the most difficult dilemmas in life.

Clearly, it is not enough for us to merely believe the
Bible. It is not enough to simply assert an innate trust in
Scriptural problem solving. It is not enough for us to blithely
assert that the ethical standard of justice revealed in the
Word of God is the only possible means to secure life, liberty,
and the pursuit of happiness. We must authenticate and vali-
date our claims. In short, we must serve, backing up Word
with deed (see James 2:14–17).

This is, after all, our Christian legacy. It was the faithful followers of Christ that launched the first hospitals, orphanages, almshouses, soup kitchens, charitable societies, relief agencies, rescue missions, hostels, and shelters. And as a result, it was the faithful followers of Christ who led Western civilization to new heights of freedom and prosperity for nearly two millennium.

The great American journalist, pastor, and statesman during the founding era, Morgan Fraser, asserted:

No tyrant can ere long rule a gracious and merciful people. Charity sows seeds of freedom that may not be suppressed, for charity naturally disposes authority to the charitable, and the charitable are naturally disposed to freedom. Thus, when the people of the Living God undertake the holy duty of caring for the needy, the poor, the brokenhearted, and the deprived, the perverse subverters of morality, truth and liberty are certain to be exposed and deposed.[11]

Stalin, Kharchev, and the Soviet leadership understood that basic truth only too well. That is why they went to such great efforts to stymie Christian service in their vast land.

If we are to be successful in developing Biblical strategies that can effectively counter the legal and cultural agenda of the ACLU, then we must begin to exercise mercy — on a comprehensive scale. We must not simply stand off life's center stage critiquing the failed and foiled attempts of others. Instead, we must fully grasp the monumental significance of Christ's assertion: "Blessed are the merciful, for they shall obtain mercy" (Matthew 5:7).

Humility

The Christian approach to any issue, or any problem, or any circumstance must always be *theocentric*. In other words, it must begin and end with — and ultimately be centered in —

the Lord. He is, after all, the *Alpha* and the *Omega* of all
things in reality (see Revelation 1:8). To attempt any approach to reality without this in view is to invite frustration
and failure. God is sovereign (see Psalm 115:3). This is the
fundamental truth that underlies the Christian *worldview*.
Thus, our lives must be suffused with a holy fear and rever-
ence of Him—to the point that everything is thereby af-
fected.

The Bible is prolific in its vehement assertion of this truth:

The fear of the Lord is the beginning of wisdom; a good
understanding have all those who do His commandments.
His praise endures forever. (Psalm 111:10)

The fear of the Lord is the beginning of knowledge, but
fools despise wisdom and instruction. (Proverbs 1:7)

The fear of the Lord prolongs days, but the years of the
wicked will be shortened. (Proverbs 10:27)

In the fear of the Lord there is strong confidence, and His
children will have a place of refuge. The fear of the Lord is
a fountain of life, to avoid the snares of death. (Proverbs
14:26–27)

Better is a little with the fear of the Lord, than great trea-
sure with trouble. (Proverbs 15:16)

Clothe yourselves in humility toward one another, for God
is opposed to the proud, but gives grace to the humble.
Humble yourselves therefore, under the mighty hand of
God, that He may lift you up in due time, casting all your
anxiety upon Him because He cares for you. (*New American Standard Bible*, 1 Peter 5:5–7)

A nation whose leaders are humbled in fear before God
will suffer no want (see Psalm 34:9). It will ever be blest (see

Psalm 115:13). It will be set high above all the nations of the earth (see Deuteronomy 28:1). Ancient Israel's greatness, in fact, can be directly attributed to her leaders' fear of God (see Deuteronomy 10:12): Abraham was a God-fearer (see Genesis 20:11); Joseph was a God-fearer (see Genesis 50:19–20); as were Job (see Job 41:23), Joshua (see Joshua 24:14), David (see 2 Samuel 23:3), Jehoshaphat (see 2 Chronicles 19:4), Hezekiah (see Jeremiah 26:19), Nehemiah (see Nehemiah 5:15), Daniel (see Daniel 9:2–19), and Jonah (see Jonah 1:9).

No headway can possibly be made toward restoring freedom and liberty in this land until just such men and women, with just such an attitude, are raised up. No amount of political finagling, judicial niggling, or cultural tinkering can effectually breach the stranglehold of iniquity and inequity in a nation where God's own people feign to humbly fear Him. As Thomas Jefferson so aptly queried: "Can the liberties of a nation be secure, when we have removed the conviction that those liberties are the gift of God?"[12]

The *Shorter Catechism* of the *Westminster Confession* properly begins by asserting that, "The chief end of man is to glorify God and to enjoy Him forever."[13] The English reformers that composed that venerable tome, recognized that the beginning of any serious endeavor must necessarily be rooted in a humble and holy fear of our Gracious and Almighty God— that worship of Him, fellowship with Him, service to Him, and communion in Him, must be the vortex of any and all other activities.

When Moses went before Pharaoh to lobby for Israel's liberty, he did not say, "Let my people go that they may start a new political party." He did not say, "Let my people go that they may establish a utopian civil structure." He did not say, "Let my people go, otherwise we're going to start several political action committees, several firebrand newsletters, and generally make your life politically intolerable." No. Instead, he said, "Let my people go, that they may hold a feast to me in the wilderness" (Exodus 5:1). And again, "Let my people go, that they may serve me in the wilderness" (Exodus 7:16). The first priority of Moses and the people was worship. It was to humble themselves before God. Then, and only then, could they move on to the other pressing matters at hand.

The Biblical faith is not simply a tool of cultural transformation — though certainly cultural transformation occurs when Christianity prevails; this is not the essence of the faith. Neither is it a political cult — though certainly the political impact of Christianity on a nation is profound whenever the people walk in its truth; this is also far from its essence. The Biblical faith is a circumspect fear of the Living God. That is its essence.

Applying this most fundamental truth to the arena of civil justice and national integrity, George Washington asserted:

> It is the first duty of all nations to acknowledge the providence of Almighty God, to obey His will, to be grateful for His benefits, and to humbly implore His protection and favor in holy fear.[14]

And, again he said:

> Of all the dispositions and habits which lead to civil prosperity, a humble fear before the Almighty and a life of Christian morality are indispensable supports. In vain would that man claim the attribute of patriotism, who should labor to subvert these great pillars of human happiness, these firmest props of the duties of men and citizens. A volume could not trace all their connections with private and public felicity. Let it simply be stated that there is no security for property, for reputation, or for life, if the sense of religious obligation deserts the oaths, which are the instruments of investigation in courts of true justice.[15]

If we are to be successful in developing Biblical strategies that can effectively counter the legal and cultural agenda of the ACLU, then we must recognize what Washington recognized. We must begin at the beginning. We must begin with God Himself — and with the fear due Him.

Statism and Personalism

The doctrine of the *separation of powers* is a cherished constitutional concept whereby each of the *separate* branches of government maintains *separate* authorities, *separate* jurisdictions, and *separate* functions. This kind of separation is the practical keystone for another hallowed constitutional concept: the doctrine of *checks and balances*. Theoretically, the judicial, legislative, and executive branches are to restrain one another from inordinate influence — and from overweening dependence upon such special interest advocacy groups as the ACLU. The founding fathers saw the separation of powers — and its corollary checks and balances — as essential for the maintenance of freedom in the new Republic.

But they were not new or original ideas. The notion of separate powers and the imposition of checks and balances did not suddenly dawn on Washington, Adams, Madison, Hamilton, Jay, and Morris. Nor were they unique to those men's mentors: Rutherford, Cromwell, Witherspoon, Smith, and Locke. Instead, the doctrines come straight out of the Bible.

Interestingly though, the idea of distinct jurisdictions and balanced institutions is not limited in the Bible simply and solely to the area of civil government. According to the Bible, the family and the church are divinely established institutions right alongside the state. Each of them has its own authority, its own jurisdiction, and its own function. Each of them is a *separate* power. And each of them is to check and balance the others.

What that means is that separation of powers and checks and balances are not simply functions of state action, Instead, they are to be carried out in contradistinction to the state by the family and the church. To center all the cultural power and activity around politics and the state is nothing more than *statism*. Even those conservatives who spend all their time and energy trying to *limit* the size and influence of the state are ultimately statist because their whole worldview is centered in the political realm. They are statists struggling for a small limited state, while liberals are struggling for a large universal state. But they are both statist. The fact is that all humanists are ultimately statists, because they have nowhere else to turn to establish life, liberty, and the pursuit of happiness than the state.

When Christians begin to believe that all or even that most of the ills of our system can be cured by more state action, or less state action, or better state action, we too, become statists. We turn Christianity into little more than a pawn of practical humanism.

The Biblical perspective of social transformation is *personal*. It includes politics. It includes influencing local government, legislators, the executive branch, the judiciary, and the bureaucracy. It includes grassroots mobilization, revitalized civic accountability, and committed community caucusing. It includes all these things. But it includes a whole lot more. And that *whole lot more* begins with the establishment of justice, mercy, and humility in our own lives, families, ministries, and churches. That *whole lot more* is not statist—centered in and around a single divine institution. It is personal. It is separated out among, and balanced between, all the divine *institutions* and the *people* that compose them.

Ultimately, what all this means is that though it is important that we develop legal strategies to combat ACLU initiatives, though we need to encourage legislation designed to restrict ACLU encroachment in the courts, and though it is necessary for us to utilize political leverage to pry the ACLU out of positions of power and influence, none of these things can be the do all and end all. Not by a long shot.

> He has shown you, O man, what is good; and what does the Lord require of you but to do justice, to love kindness, and to walk humbly with your God. (Micah 6:8)

Conclusion

George Washington, in one of his final statements to the young nation that he had taken such a pivotal role in establishing, said:

> I now make it my earnest prayer, that God would most graciously be pleased to dispose us all, to do justice, to love mercy, and to demean ourselves with that charity, humility, and pacific temper of mind, which were the characteristics of the Divine Author of our blessed religion, for without an humble imitation and example in these things, we can never hope to be a happy nation.[16]

He understood only too well that in order to secure life, liberty, and the pursuit of happiness in this land, a foundation had to be laid first—a foundation rooted in the three disciplines exposited by the Old Testament prophet Micah: justice, mercy, and humility. He understood that if we are to be repairers of the breach—the breach of freedom and hope in our land—then we must begin at the beginning.

> Is this not the fast that I have chosen: to loose the bonds of wickedness, to undo the heavy burdens, to let the oppressed go free, and that you break every yoke? Is it not to share your bread with the hungry, and that you bring to your house the poor who are cast out; when you see the naked, that you cover him, and not hide yourself from your own flesh? Then your light shall break forth like the morning, your healing shall spring forth speedily, and your righteousness shall go before you; the glory of the LORD shall be your rear guard. Then you shall call, and the LORD will answer; you shall cry, and He will say, "Here I am." If you take away the yoke from your midst, the pointing of the finger, and speaking wickedness, if you extend your soul to the hungry and satisfy the afflicted soul, then your light shall dawn in the darkness, and your darkness shall be as the noonday. The LORD will guide you continually, and sat-

isfy your soul in drought, and strengthen your bones; you shall be like a watered garden, and like a spring of water, whose waters do not fail. Those from among you shall build the old waste places; you shall raise up the foundations of many generations; and *you shall be called the Repairer of the Breach*, the Restorer of Streets to Dwell In. (Isaiah 58:6–12)

TAKING ACTION

in operibus sit abundantia mea[1]

O nce we have been thoroughly informed by a Christian worldview, and once justice, mercy, and humility have been ably translated into our lives, families, ministries, and churches, then any number of practical steps can be taken in the civil sphere as well to directly dilute the effects of the ACLU and restore our once stalwart heritage.

There was, after all, once a time when the American court system was the greatest friend of Christendom in the entire culture. Just based on its history, no one could have ever predicted its current nasty temper. Flag burning, Christian bashing, school thrashing, baby killing, perversion flaunting, and crime baiting were crimes to be punished not rights to be protected.

That was because the Christian worldview informed the presuppositional base of the American legal system — and justice, mercy, and humility informed its *modus operandi*.

In upholding the Northwest Ordinance of 1787, the Supreme Court boldly, and without the least hesitation, asserted that: "Religion, morality, and knowledge, being necessary to good government and the happiness of mankind, schools and the means of righteous education should forever be encouraged."[2]

In 1791, the Court upheld the right of five ratifying states to officially protest the omission of a direct mention of God in the new Constitution saying: "Indeed the concern of the Christian status of the nation is well founded."[3]

In 1825, the Court refused to hear complaints over a trade treaty between the U.S. and Czarist Russia that began with the words, "In the Name of the Most Holy and Indivisible Trinity."[4] The opinion simply rebuffed the criticisms, saying the treaty's preamble was "entirely legitimate."[5]

In 1844, the Court argued in Vidol v. Girard that:

> Christianity is part of our common law. Its divine origin and truth are admitted and therefore it is not to be maliciously and openly reviled and blasphemed against, to the annoyance of believers or the injury of the public.[6]

In 1892, the Court stated in a celebrated case against the federal government that:

> No purpose of action against religion can be imputed to any legislation, state or national, because this is a religious people. This is historically true. From the discovery of this continent to the present hour, there is a single voice making this affirmation.[7]

Again in 1930, the Court reiterated that position in the case of McIntosh v. U.S. saying:

> We are a Christian people, according to our motto. The right of religious freedom, demands acknowledgment, with reverence, the duty of obedience to the will of God.[8]

And in 1952, the Court argued in Zorack v. Clauson that: "We are a religious people whose institutions presuppose a Supreme Being."[9]

Sadly, that great legacy has been thoroughly eroded. The courts have yielded to the rhetoric and pressures of the likes of the ACLU and thus have been transformed from being friends of the faith into the enemies of the faith. And that has in turn meant that the courts have been transformed from being the friends of liberty into the enemies of liberty. Under the guise of *pluralism*, the courts have manipulated our great heritage of freedom through ethical justice into a *carte blanche* for the ACLU's humanistic proponents of an officially atheist and statist system.

And now, because the courts so dominate the American legal scene,[10] if there is to be any hope of restoring our cultural heritage and reversing our moral losses, we are going to have to begin with them.

So, what can we do?

First, we need to encourage one another to become informed and willing jurors. The purpose of a jury is to put a check on the power of the magistrates by putting ultimate power in the hands of individual citizens. The Constitution affords each of us with three *votes:* first, in free elections in order to choose our representatives; second in the Grand Jury in order to restrain overzealous public prosecutors; and third, in jury trials in order to restrain the courts from unjustly applying legitimate laws or from legitimately applying unjust laws. Thus, the true function of a jury is to try not only the actions and the motives of the defendant, but the actions and the motives of the prosecution, the court, and the statute as well.

As Christians, we need to *aspire* to jury duty, not *avoid* it. We need to apply ourselves diligently so that we can be selected. We need to be certain never to disqualify ourselves in pro-life cases, or pornography cases, or child abuse cases just because we hold moral convictions on those matters. Moral conviction is *exactly* what the courts need right now.

If a Christian presence is never felt on trial juries, there is little hope that the influence of the ACLU will ever be counterbalanced with moral uprightness.

Second, we need to formulate an offensive program of litigation. There is no reason why the ACLU should be the only one to take cases before the courts as a means of policy advocacy. There is no reason why the ACLU should be the only one to utilize manipulated test cases as a means of establishing legal precedents.

For several years now, we have been fighting what has for all intents and purposes been a defensive war for liberty and freedom — whenever churches, or parents, or home schoolers, or pro-lifers, or Christian students, or gun owners, or property owners, or small businessmen have been attacked or harassed by the likes of the ACLU, we have tried to respond with an able legal defense. And this has staved off the discriminatory persecution to some degree. But, the *best* defense is a good offense.

We need to begin to target particular statutes in particular jurisdictions with particular judges reversing some of the ACLU's inroads into the life and health of our communities. We need to begin to plot long term legal strategies. And we need to aggressively preserve and conserve those liberties that we have been able to retain.

Third, we need to be actively involved in civic affairs, including the political process. Not only do we need to *vote*, we need to participate in the precinct process. We need to contact our magistrates concerning key issues. We need to get involved in the campaigns of candidates that we favor. We need to make ourselves available to testify at committee and sub-committee hearings. We need to launch educational programs, petition drives, letter writing campaigns, media blitzes, PAC initiatives, and grassroots referendums. In other words, we need to be involved in the *whole* process of shaping and directing the civic sphere.[11] If we don't — or won't — the ACLU certainly will.

The legislative process is the source of all federal law. The courts cannot make law, they can only rule on already existing statutes — although sometimes that is a bit difficult to tell. Only the combined efforts of the two branches of Congress — the House of Representatives and the Senate — can make law.

As presently constituted, the House has four hundred thirty-five members apportioned on the basis of population, and elected every two years from among the fifty states. The Senate has one hundred members, two from each state, elected to staggered six-year terms. Those five hundred thirty-five magistrates have the power — through direct legislation and through wise and discerning court appointments — to put an end to government discrimination against Christians, stop abortion, outlaw pornography, restrain educational repression, check judicial activism, transform the criminal justice system, and minimize the impact of the ACLU and other radical left-wing advocacy groups all the while preserving life, liberty, and the pursuit of happiness. They could bring balance once again to our judicial system. If only they would.

And indeed, they *would* if we would only exercise the right kind of influence and bring the right kind of pressure to bear — if only we *would* get involved.

Fourth, we need to begin to exercise all our constitutional options to check and balance the various branches of government. Not only do we need to be involved in the civil sphere in order to insure that faithful and clearheaded magistrates represent us in the corridors of power and influence, we need to make certain that they utilize their energies and efforts wisely. Congress can for instance, limit the jurisdiction of the courts in key areas. According to the Constitution, the Supreme Court has original jurisdiction only in cases where ambassadors and consuls are involved, or in cases in which an individual state is a party. In any other situation, Congress need only pass a resolution removing the Supreme Court's appellate jurisdiction over certain issues with a fifty percent plus one vote of those present in both chambers.[12] In that way, the ACLU's strategy of utilizing the courts to institute its radical agenda of cultural transformation would be entirely short-circuited. So for instance, the courts would have no appellate jurisdiction over abortion cases say, or perhaps over flag burning cases, or even over obscenity standards established by local communities.

Fifth, we need to contain and restrain the lumbering government bureaucracy. The bureaucracy is perhaps the most powerful *branch* of the American governmental system. It is without question the largest and most expensive. And this, despite the fact that it is not even *mentioned* in the Constitution.

That can make for a very dangerous situation. After all, who monitors the bureaucracy? Who checks and balances its administration? Who even knows what it does? Turning out thousands of pages of regulations, rulings, and guidelines every week dealing with the application of court judgments, civil litigation, legislative enforcement, and civil administration with very little accountability, makes the bureaucracy a perfect arena of operations for the likes of the ACLU—especially when all other avenues of legal recourse have closed.

The key then for bringing the bureaucracy back into line is accountability. We must erase the anonymity of civil servants. We must eliminate what is all too often, their nameless faceless status. We need to penetrate the thick insulation of red tape and find out who is responsible for what, when, where, and why—and then hold them accountable.

Sixth, we need to educate the public. We need to disseminate information about the crucial issues of our day, about various court precedents, and about the ACLU so that the citizenry is not bamboozled by the organization's fine sounding rhetoric. By distributing books, tapes, and, pamphlets, by writing articles, newsletters, and op-ed pieces, by commenting at community meetings, hearings, and caucuses, by informing newspapers, television stations, and radio broadcasters, and by any and every other means at our disposal, we need to make the issues clear.

People need to know what is at stake. If we don't tell them, who will? Certainly not the ACLU.

One way or another, we must stem the tide of humanism in our courts and in our culture. One way or another, we must halt the ACLU juggernaut in its tracks. One way or another, we must take action. It appears that it is now or never.

ACLU FACTS

hagia sophia[1]

A lthough most of the following material may be found elsewhere in the body of the book, it is reproduced here in a condensed format for easy reference. For exact references and the full context of each fact or quote, see the end notes to the main text.

Basic Background

- The organization was founded as the *Bureau for Conscientious Objectors* of the American Union Against Militarism in 1917 by Roger Baldwin.

- The name was changed to the *Civil Liberties Bureau* later that year.

- It separated from the AUAM and became the *National Civil Liberties Bureau* in October of that same year.

- On August 31, 1918 the Bureau was raided by the FBI searching for evidence of subversive materials.

- On November 11, 1918 Baldwin began serving a one year term in a Federal prison for sedition.

- Upon his release he renamed the Bureau, the *American Civil Liberties Union*, on January 20, 1920.

- Today, it maintains a membership of 250,00 members, with seventy staff lawyers, and 5,000 volunteer attorneys, handling an average of 6,000 cases at any one time, with an annual budget of fourteen million dollars.

- Much of that budget is supplied by the American taxpayer through the Federal program mandated by the Civil Rights Attorneys' Fee Awards Act of 1976.

Philosophical Roots

- According to Baldwin, "We are for Socialism, disarmament, and ultimately for abolishing the state itself as an instrument of violence and compulsion. We seek the social ownership of property, the abolition of the propertied class, and the sole control of those who produce wealth. Communism is the goal."

- Several of the original Executive Board members besides Baldwin, including William Foster, Elizabeth Gurley Flynn, and Louis Budenez, were later prominent leaders of the Communist Party USA.

- Even today, the National Board reads like a Who's Who of the American Left: George McGovern, Norman Lear, Ed Asner, Julian Bond, Carl Sagan, Susan Estrich, Patricia Schroeder, Kurt Vonnegut, Norman Cousins, Ramsey Clark, Harriet Pilpel, Birch Bayh, Henry Steel Commager, Arthur Schlessenger, Lowell Weicker, Burt Lancaster, Ira Glasser, Alan Reitman, Norman Dorsen, Morton Halperin, and Sissy Farenthold.

- According to the Union's *First Annual Report*, it was a part of the "center of resistance" in American society, which also included "the IWW and the Communist Party."

- That report called the Union, "a militant, central bureau in the labor movement for legal aid, defense strategy, information, and propaganda."

- It went on to argue that "standards of civil liberty cannot be attained as abstract principles or as constitutional guarantees — economic power is necessary to assert and maintain all rights."

- A later report stated that, "the struggle between capital and labor is the most vital application of the principle of civil liberty."

- According to a committee of the New York State Legislature, "The ACLU, in the last analysis, is a supporter of all subversive movements; its propaganda is detrimental to the interests of the state. Its main work is to uphold the Communists in spreading revolutionary propaganda and inciting revolutionary activities to undermine our American institutions and overthrow our Federal government."

- According to an investigative committee of the U.S. Congress, long before the days of the "Red Scare" in Washington, "The ACLU is closely affiliated with the Communist movement in the United States, and fully ninety percent of its efforts are on behalf of Communists who have come into conflict with the law. It claims to stand for free speech, free press, and free assembly, but it is quite apparent that the main function of the ACLU is to attempt to protect the Communists in their advocacy of force and violence to overthrow the government."

- Baldwin, in writing about the Soviet Union, argued, "Such an attitude as I express toward the relation of economic to civil liberty may easily be construed as condoning in Russia repressions which I condemn in Capitalist countries. It is true that I feel differently about them, because I regard them as unlike. Repressions in Western Democracies are violations of professed constitutional liberties, and I condemn them as such. Repressions in Soviet Russia are weapons of struggle in a transition period to Socialism. The society the Communists seek to create will be freed of class struggle — if achieved — and therefore of repression."

- Later, he wrote, "All my associates in the struggle for civil liberties take a class position, though many don't know it. I too take a class position. It is anti-capitalist and pro-revolutionary. We champion civil liberty as the best of the non-violent means of building the power on which the worker's rule must be based. If we aid the reactionaries to get free speech now and then, if we go outside the class struggle to fight censorship, it is only because those liberties help to create a more hospitable atmosphere for working-class liberties. The class struggle is the central conflict of the world; all others are incidental."

- Again, he wrote, "When that power of the working class is once achieved, as it has been only in the Soviet Union, we are for maintaining it by any means whatever."

Issues

- The ACLU takes the position that all pornography — including child porn should be "fully and completely protected as free speech" by the First Amendment (Policy 4).

- It opposes the rating of music and movies (Policy 18).

- It opposes any kind of discretionary judgment concerning homosexuals — including in foster care or custody cases (Policy 264).

- It advocates the legalization of prostitution (Policy 211).

- It advocates the decriminalization and legalization of all drugs and controlled substances (Policy 210).

- It opposes parental consent of minor treatment at abortion and birth control clinics (Policy 262).

- It opposes informed consent preceding abortion procedures (Policy 263).

- It opposes spousal consent preceding abortion procedures (Policy 262).

- It has stridently fought for an extension of Federal welfare programs and services — including means-tested entitlement day care, housing, and personal income — despite their destructiveness to the nuclear family (Policy 318).

- It has consistently opposed the right of parents to choose the schools their children attend through any sort of a voucher system (Policy 80).

- It opposes the right of communities to conduct any sort of sobriety road checks (Policy 217).

- It opposes the right of private physicians and dentists to trace AIDS transmission or to notify unsuspecting persons that they may be in danger of infection (Policy 268).

- It opposes right of communities to use metal detectors in airports as a deterrent against terrorism (Policy 270).

- It opposes the right of communities to impose restrictions on welfare subsidies (Policy 318).

- It advocates tax funded abortion and birth limitation services, unilateral disarmament, disinvestment in South Africa, gun control, fluoridation in water supplies, enfranchisement of illegal aliens, euthanasia, polygamy, government control of church institutions, and a whole host of other Leftist notions (Policies 263, 133, 402, 47, 261, 323, 271, 91, and 85).

- It has even argued, "that teaching monogamous, heterosexual intercourse within marriage is a traditional American value is an unconstitutional establishment of a religious doctrine," and therefore "violates the First Amendment" (CA CLU).

ORGANIZATIONAL RESOURCES

bona opera[1]

T here are a number of excellent organizations that either provide information or legal aid in the area of civil liberties and constitutional rights. These groups are not only helping to preserve our liberties by going head-to-head against the ACLU in our communities and courtrooms, they are also providing positive leadership and direction wherever deficiencies exist in our present legislative and litigal systems:

- Accuracy in Media
  1275 K Street, NW
  Washington, DC 20005

- American Family Association
  P.O. Drawer 2440
  Tupelo, MS 38803

- Christian Action Council
  422 C St., NE
  Washington, DC 20002

- Christian Legal Society
  P.O. Box 1492
  Merrifield, VA 22116

- Committee to Protect the Family
  8001 Forbes Place, Suite 102
  Springfield, VA 22151

- Concerned Women for America
  122 C St., NW, Suite 800
  Washington, DC 20001

- Eagle Forum
  P.O. Box 618
  Alton, IL 62002

- Family of the Americas Foundation
  P.O. Box 219
  Mandeville, LA 70448

- Family Research Council
  515 Second St., NE
  Washington, DC 20002

- Focus on the Family
  801 Corporate Center Drive
  Pomona, CA 91764

- Free Congress Research and Education Foundation
  721 Second St., NE
  Washington, DC 20002

- Gun Owners of America
  8001 Forbes Place, Suite 102
  Springfield, VA 22151

- Heritage Foundation
  214 Massachusetts Ave. N.E.
  Washington, DC 20002

- Institute for Christian Economics
  P.O. Box 8000
  Tyler, TX 75711

- Legal Affairs Council
  Freedom Plaza
  Chantilly, VA 22021

- National Right to Life Committee
  419 7th St., NW, Suite 402
  Washington, DC 20004

- National Right to Work Committee
  8001 Braddock Road
  Springfield, VA 22160

- Operation Rescue
  P.O. Box 1180
  Binghamton, NY 13902

- Pacific Legal Foundation
  555 Capitol Mall, Suite 350
  Sacramento, CA 95814

- The Plymouth Rock Foundation
  P.O. Box 577
  Marlborough, NH 03455

- Rutherford Institute
  P.O. Box 510
  Manassas, VA 22110

- Washington Legal Foundation
  1205 N Street N.W.
  Washington, DC 20036

BIBLIOGRAPHIC RESOURCES

boniface[1]

There are a number of very helpful in-depth studies available that throw a much needed spotlight on the issues raised in this book in general and the ACLU in particular. Among the best are:

William A. Donohue, *The Politics of the American Civil Liberties Union,* (New Brunswick, NJ: Transaction Books, 1985).

Daniel L. Dreisbach, *Real Threat and Mere Shadow,* (Westchester, IL: Crossway Books, 1987).

John W. Whitehead, *The Separation Illusion,* (Milford, MI: Mott Media, 977).

John W. Whitehead, *The Stealing of America,* (Westchester, IL: Crossway Books, 1983).

Other related studies that would be helpful in sorting out the issues of liberty and justice — including all those consulted during the research and writing of this book — would compose a prohibitively large list. Therefore only a very select list is provided here for the reader to pursue for advanced study:

Peggy Lamson, *Roger Baldwin: Founder of the American Civil Liberties Union,* (Boston: Houghton Mifflin, 1976).

William H. McIlhany, *The ACLU on Trial,* (New Rochelle, NY: Arlington House, 1976).

Norman Dorsen, ed., *Our Endangered Rights: The ACLU Report on Civil Liberties Today,* (New York: Pantheon Books, 1984).

Thomas I. Emerson, ed., *Political and Civil Rights in the United States,* 2 vols., (Boston: Little, Brown, and Co., 1967).

Elizabeth Dilling, *The Red Network: A Who's Who and Handbook of Radicalism for Patriots,* (Chicago: Dilling Press, 1934).

Richard Neely, *How the Courts Govern America,* (New Haven, CN: Yale University Press, 1981).

Paul L. Murphy, *World War I and the Origin of Civil Liberties,* (New York: W. W. Norton, 1979).

Arthur S. Link and Richard L. McCormick, *Progressivism,* (Arlington Heights, IL: Harlan Davidson, 1983).

John C. Calhoun, *A Disquisition on Government,* (Indianapolis, IN: Bobbs-Merrill Co., 1853, 1981).

Robert H. Montgomery, *Sacco-Vanzetti: The Murder and the Myth,* (New York: Devin-Adair, 1960).

Barbara Hobenstreit, *Eternal Vigilance: The ACLU,* (New York: J. Messner, 1971).

Charles Colson and Daniel Van Ness, *Convicted: New Hope for Ending America's Crime Crisis,* (Westchester, IL: Crossway Books, 1989).

Charles E. Silberman, *Criminal Violence, Criminal Justice,* (New York: Vintage Books, 1980).

Charles Hyneman and Donald Lutz, *American Political Writing During the Founding Era: 1760–1805,* (Indianapolis, IN: Liberty Press, 1983).

David Bollier, *Liberty and Justice for Some: Defending a Free Society from the Radical Right's Holy War on Democracy*, (Washington, DC: People for the American Way, 1982).

Marvin Olasky, *Patterns of Corporate Philanthropy: Public Affairs Giving and the Forbes 100*, (Washington, DC: Capital Research Center, 1987).

William S. Lind and William H. Marshner, *Cultural Conservatism: Toward a New National Agenda*, (Washington, DC: Institute for Cultural Conservatism, 1987).

Gary North, *Victim's Rights: A Biblical View*, (Tyler, TX: Institute for Christian Economics, 1989).

Robert Nisbet, *The History of the Idea of Progress*, (New York: Basic Books, 1980).

Paul Johnson, *Intellectuals*, (New York: Harper and Row, 1988).

Thomas I. Emerson, David Haber, and Norman Dorsen, *Political and Civil Rights in the United States*, (Boston, MS: Little, Brown, and Company, 1967).

Peter Waldron, *Rebuilding the Walls: A Biblical Strategy for Restoring America's Greatness*, (Brentwood, TN: Wolgemuth and Hyatt, Publishers, 1987).

END NOTES

ACKNOWLEDGEMENTS

1. Paul Johnson, *Intellectuals*, (New York: Harper and Row, 1989), 82.
2. See especially, William A. Donohue, *The Politics of the American Civil Liberties Union*, (New Brunswick, NJ: Transaction Press, 1985).
3. A complete bibliography of helpful resources from these diligent researchers, writers, and workers is provided in Appendix C.
4. From St. Ephrem's "Harp of the Spirit," translated and edited in F. Forrester Church and Terrence J. Mulry, *The Macmillan Book of Earliest Christian Hymns*, (New York: Macmillan, 1988), 155.

INTRODUCTION

1. "Something supernatural in the disease."
2. Hilaire Belloc, *Notes of a Curmudgeon*, (London: Albright's Ltd., 1956), 11.
3. G.K. Chesterton, *The Man Who Was Thursday*, (Geneva: Palling Reprint Classics, 1908, 1961), p. xii.
4. In the past, my work has been written in such a way that it could be understood on several levels simultaneously—so that it can be grasped by the average reader, while at the same time providing challenges for the advanced student. This book is no exception. My aim has been partly to inform, partly to motivate, partly to strategize, and partly to stimulate. But in addition, it has been partly to entertain literarily. Understanding this literary backdrop is by no means necessary to grasp the message of this book. And it is by no means intended to distract the reader from assimilating information about the ACLU—in fact, if this aspect of the book is even noticeable to the reader, then the artistic endeavor has actually failed. It has been included simply because I believe

that writing is not simply the transmission of data. It is an art—
even when it takes the form of non-fiction.

5. John Frame, *Medical Ethics: Principles, Persons, and Problems*,
(Phillipsburg, NJ: Presbyterian and Reformed, 1988), 4.

CHAPTER 1: NIGHTMARE ON MAIN STREET

1. Hilaire Belloc, *The Path to Rome*, (New York: Penguin Books,
1958), 66.

2. G.K. Chesterton, *Orthodoxy*, (New York: Dodd, Mead, and Company, 1908), 74–75.

3. "But let this induce you to go on more boldly."

4. Belloc, 74.

5. Chesterton, 25.

6. This story first appeared in the *East Texas Federation for Decency
Newsletter*, August, 1988.

7. This story first appeared in the *Loyola Mothers Against Drunk
Driving News*, Winter 1987.

8. This story first appeared in the *Journal of Non-Registered Churches
and Charities*, vol. 2, no. 1.

9. For more on the role of Planned Parenthood in the deception of
parents and teens alike see, George Grant, *Grand Illusions: The
Legacy of Planned Parenthood*, (Brentwood, TN: Wolgemuth and
Hyatt, 1988).

10. For more on the complications of abortion, see Grant, 65–74.

11. This story first appeared in the *Talumma Crisis Pregnancy Help
Center Update*, November, 1987.

12. This story first appeared in the *Seventh Trumpet Newsletter*, October, 1987.

13. This story first appeared in the *Pro-Life Action News Briefs*, September, 1988.

14. This story first appeared in the *BridgeBuilder Magazine*,
March/April, 1989.

15. This story first appeared in the *Operation Rescue of Pittsburgh
Press Release*, March 14, 1989.

16. Our court system is so construed that there are no longer any
"winners." Everyone who gets involved in litigation "loses." Even
the "mere threat" of a lawsuit—as in several of the cases in this
chapter—can be devastating to the finances and well-being of a
family, a business, or a community.

17. Obviously, the ACLU is able to wield much of its power outside the courtroom simply through counsel, notification, warnings, and intimidation. Each of the cases in this chapter was chosen to demonstrate that very point. You'll notice that none of them are exactly precedent setting Supreme Court cases. Instead, they are quiet, unspectacular situations exploited by ACLU-affiliated lawyers — or their proxies — to accomplish their own political or ideological ends.

CHAPTER 2: A VERY RESPECTABLE HERESY

1. "The tongue persuades, the life commands."
2. Hilaire Belloc, *The Path to Rome*, (New York: Penguin Books, 1958), 91.
3. G.K. Chesterton, *Heretics*, (New York: Devin Adair, 1950), 23.
4. *Political Demographics Journal*, December, 1988.
5. This often repeated sobriquet for the ACLU first made its appearance in the Spring 1986 newsletter of the Texas Civil Liberties Union, in an article written by the state affiliate's executive director, Gara LaMarche.
6. *The Boston Globe*, May 15, 1981.
7. Ibid.
8. *Investigation of Communist Propaganda*, House Report 2290, Seventy-First Congress, Third Session, January 17, 1931.
9. *Does the ACLU Serve the Communist Cause?*, General Report, American Legion Posts 1 and 51, Phoenix, Arizona, 1965.
10. Mike Boos, *When Will They Stop?*, (Chantilly, VA: Legal Affairs Council, 1989).
11. *AFA Journal*, November/December, 1988.
12. *Compromise With Injustice*, Release 22, 1961.
13. *The ACLU: Friend or Foe*, Special Report, 1983.
14. H. Edward Rowe, *The ACLU and America's Freedoms*, (Washington: Church League of America, 1984).
15. A.C. Maricopa, *The ACLU and Communism*, (Scottsdale, AZ: National Advisory Council, 1964).
16. *American Opinion Magazine*, September, 1969.
17. *Accuracy in Media Report*, November, 1988.
18. *The Washington Times*, October 29, 1982.
19. *Operation Rescue News Brief*, March 10, 1989.

20. Franklin V. York, "The ACLU Con Game," *The Review of the News*, August 13, 1975.

21. See, for instance, David Shaw, "The Rift in the ACLU's Ranks," *The Los Angeles Times*, October 5, 1973; and, Abraham Isserman, "Uncivil Liberties in the ACLU," *The Daily World Magazine*, October 22, 1977.

22. See Corliss Lamont, *Yes to Life: The Memoirs of Corliss Lamont*, (New York: Horizon Press, 1981).

23. See, Peggy Lamson, *Roger Baldwin: The Founder of the American Civil Liberties Union*, (Boston: Houghton Mifflin Company, 1976), 1–13.

24. Quoted from the testimony of Senator Clark in *The Congressional Record*, June 13, 1962, 9563.

25. Ibid.

26. Ibid.

27. Ibid.

28. *Civil Liberties*, Februrary, 1964.

29. *ACLU Annual Report*, 1977, 1.

30. William Reece Smith, Jr., President of the American Bar Association, quoted in "Guardian of Liberty," *ACLU Briefing Paper, Number One*, 1988, 1.

31. Quoted in A.C. Germann, "Two Sides of Every Coin," *The Professional Police Journal*, March/April, 1962.

32. Ibid.

33. Ibid.

34. Ibid.

35. *Civil Liberties Review*, March/April, 1978, 47.

36. William A. Donohue, *The Politics of the American Civil Liberties Union*, (New Brunswick, NJ: Transaction Books, 1985), 2.

37. Nat Hentoff, "The Enemy Within the ACLU," *Sweet land of Liberty*, November, 1988, 2.

38. Richard and Susan Vigilante, "Taking Liberties: The ACLU Strays From Its Mission," *Policy Review*, September, 1988, 28.

39. *Insight Magazine*, March 21, 1988, 13.

40. *The Kansas City Star*, June 18, 1989.

41. Martin Lambert Sess, *Enemies of Liberty*, (Dallas, TX: Investment Strategy Publications Bureau, 1982), 188.

42. *ACLU Annual Report*, 1984–1985, 8–16.

43. Although the ACLU was not chartered in its present form until January 1920, it had existed in various other guises ever since

Roger Nash Baldwin came to New York and established the Bureau for Conscientious Objectors for the American Union Against Militarism in 1917. See Chapter Four for further details.

44. *ACLU Annual Report*, 1986–1987, 18.
45. Compared with the supporting memberships of Phyllis Schlafley's Eagle Forum, Beverly LaHaye's Concerned Women for America, Jerry Nim's Moral Majority, Jerry Falwell's Liberty Federation, Don Wildmon's American Family Federation, Randall Terry's Operation Rescue, James Dobson's Focus on the Family, Pat Robertson's 700 Club, D. James Kennedy's Coral Ridge Ministries, and John Whitehead's Rutherford Institute, the ACLU membership is minuscule at best.
46. *ACLU Annual Report*, 1986–1987, 16–18.
47. *Insight Magazine*, March 21, 1988, 15.
48. *The New York Times*, October 2, 1988.
49. Quoted in a fund raising letter from Barry Steinhardt, Executive Director, ACLU of Pennsylvania, Spring 1986.
50. As an example of this kind of influence see the case examples in Chapter One.
51. At this point, it may be wise to define more clearly what I mean by the word "heresy." According to the dictionary, it is "an opinion or doctrine at variance with established beliefs; adherence to such unorthodox opinion." In the American moral, political, and legal arena in which the ACLU has its stock and trade, "heresy" is simply the contravening of the established standards of Western Civilization and the Scriptural Revelation upon which that Civilization has been built. For a complete description of how the ACLU qualifies as a "heresy," see Chapter Three.
52. *ACLU Annual Report*, 1920, 1.
53. Stephen Halpern, "Assessing the Litigative Role of ACLU Chapters," in Stephen L. Wasby, ed., *Civil Liberties: Policy and Policy Making*, (Lexington, MA: Lexington Books, 1976), 159–167.
54. *Insight Magazine*, March 21, 1988.
55. *ACLU Annual Report*, 1986–1987, 16–17.
56. Although the national ACLU shares financially with its affiliates, the local groups generally have expenses well above and beyond what this "cooperative program" could ever possibly provide.
57. Halpern, 160–161.
58. Quoted in Paul Johnson, *Intellectuals*, (New York: Harper and Row, 1989), 23.

59. *Insight Magazine*, March 21, 1988.
60. *Council Focus and News*, December, 1988.
61. Lamson, 232.
62. For more on the tactical agenda of Baalism in ancient Israel, see Carlos Ortiz-Maya, trans. Michael K. Harnell, *Baalism*, (London: Blackstone and Welterwood, 1977), 134–145.
63. See James Billington, *Fire in the Minds of Men: Origins of the Revolutionary Faith*, (New York: Basic Books, 1980).
64. Johnson, 269.
65. This concept will be examined in detail in Chapter Eleven.

CHAPTER 3: LAW, LIBERTY, AND LICENSE

1. Hilaire Belloc, *The Servile State*, (London: T.N. Foulis, 1913), 58.
2. G.K. Chesterton, *Orthodoxy*, (New York: Dodd, Mead, and Company, 1908), 19.
3. "Care nothing for their lies."
4. Belloc, 58.
5. Chesterton, 43.
6. Quoted in, Jon Winokur, ed., *The Portable Curmudgeon*, (New York: New American Library, 1987), 12.
7. Quoted in, William Thayer-Noyes, *Anecdotal Evidence*, (London: Charing Cross Printers, 1979), 36.
8. Ibid, 37.
9. Nat Hentoff, "The Enemy Within the ACLU," *Sweet Land of Liberty*, n.d.
10. *ACLU Annual Report*, 1986–1987, 10.
11. William A. Donohue, *The Politics of the American Civil Liberties Union*, (New Brunswick, NJ: Transaction Books, 1985), 36.
12. Ibid.
13. *Civil Liberty: A Statement defining the Position of the ACLU on the issues in the United States Today*, July, 1920.
14. Ibid, 39.
15. Ibid, 94.
16. See, *The Washington Times*, October 29, 1982; and Norman Dorsen, ed., *Our Endangered Rights: The ACLU Report on Civil Liberties Today*, (New York: Pantheon Books, 1984).
17. *The Wall Street Journal*, October 20, 1988.
18. *The New York Times*, October 2, 1988.
19. *ACLU Briefing Paper*, no. 1, 1987, 1.

20. Ibid.
21. Quoted in Peggy Lamson, *Roger Baldwin: Founder of the American Civil Liberties Union*, (Boston: Houghton Mifflin, 1976), 192.
22. Donohue, 5–6.
23. *Policy Guide of the American Civil Liberties Union*, 1986, 222–232.
24. Ibid, 242–244.
25. Ibid, 434.
26. *Insight Magazine*, March 21, 1988.
27. *San Francisco Chronicle*, October 5, 1973.
28. *The Boston Globe*, February 27, 1984.
29. *Insight Magazine*, March 21, 1988.
30. Donohue, 5.
31. Ibid.
32. Ibid, 4.
33. *The New York Times*, October 2, 1988.
34. *ACLU Annual Report*, 1984–1985, 1.
35. Donohue, 49.
36. Ibid.
37. Ibid, 51.
38. *Policy Guide*, 95.
39. *ACLU Annual Report*, 1984–1985, 6.
40. It has often sided with those who wish to "prohibit the free exercise" of the Christian faith. See, *The Washington Times*, October 29, 1982.
41. In the Watergate impeachment case, the ACLU proposed that President Nixon waive his right to refrain from incriminating testimony and that President Ford be stripped of his pardoning powers; See, *The Boston Globe*, September 12, 1974.
42. *The Butler Eagle*, September 28, 1970.
43. *Operation Rescue News Brief*, March, 1989.
44. *Policy Guide*, 98–99.
45. Ibid, 100–101.
46. Donohue, 50.
47. *ACLU Annual Report*, 1986–1987, 6.
48. Ibid, 9.
49. Ibid.
50. *Policy Guide*, 334–361.
51. Ibid.
52. Ibid.
53. Donohue, 102–103.

54. *Crossbow Magazine*, Spring, 1978.
55. *Insight Magazine*, March 21, 1988.
56. *Conservative Digest*, December, 1988.
57. *Operation Rescue Newsbrief*, March, 1989.
58. *The Boston Herald*, April 6, 1988.
59. Janet Benshoof, et al., *Preserving the Right to Choose: How to Cope with Violence and Disruption at Abortion Clinics*, (New York: ACLU Reproductive Freedom Project, 1986), 34–35; and, Janet Benshoof, et al., *Parental Notice Laws: Their Catastrophic Impact on Teenagers' Right to Abortion*, (New York: ACLU Reproductive Freedom Project, 1986), 8–9.
60. *Pittsburgh Post-Gazette*, September 22, 1981.
61. *The Wall Street Journal*, October 20, 1988.
62. *ACLU Briefing Paper*, no. 1, 1987.
63. *Goals for 1961*, ACLU brochure, 1960.
64. *Commentary*, January, 1989.
65. Donohue, 105.
66. *Policy Guide*, 403–409.
67. Donohue, 80.
68. *Policy Guide*, 380–382.
69. *The Wall Street Journal*, October 20, 1988.
70. *The Wall Street Journal*, October 3, 1988.
71. Donohue, 77.
72. Ibid, 77.
73. Ibid.
74. See, George Grant, *Bringing in the Sheaves: Transforming Poverty into Productivity*, (Brentwood, TN: Wolgemuth and Hyatt, 1988).
75. *Policy Review*, September, 1988.
76. *The Wall Street Journal*, October 3, 1988.
77. This kind of hyperbole can be seen in Ira Glasser's overstated "Executive Director's Message" in, *ACLU Annual Report*, 1986–1987, 8–9.
78. *Policy Guide*, 6–9.
79. Ibid, 161–162.
80. Ibid, 260, 265.
81. Ibid, 246–249, 267.
82. Barry Lynn, "Memo on Witchcraft Amendment to the Appropriations Bill," ACLU Washington Office, October 10, 1985.
83. Ibid, 176–177.
84. Ibid, 261.

85. Ibid, 185–187.
86. Ibid, 245–248.
87. Ibid, 347–348.
88. Ibid, 345.
89. Ibid, 345–346.
90. Ibid, 376–379.
91. Ibid, 159–160.
92. *Conservative Digest*, December, 1988.
93. Ibid, 191–221.
94. *ACLU Policy Guide*, 307–309.
95. Ibid, 307–308.
96. Ibid, 85–90.
97. *Operation Rescue Newsbriefs*, March, 1989.
98. Ibid, 175.
99. Quoted from a letter sent to the California Assembly Education Committee by the ACLU California Legislative Office, May 26, 1988.
100. *The Wall Street Journal*, October 20, 1988.
101. *Houston Chronicle*, March 14, 1979.
102. *Accuracy in Media Report*, November, 1988.
103. *The New York Times Magazine*, June 19, 1966.
104. *ACLU Briefing Paper*, no. 1, 1987.
105. *Accuracy in Media Report*, November, 1988.
106. *The Wall Street Journal*, March 29, 1965.
107. *Civil Liberties*, May, 1961.
108. *World Magazine*, November 21,1988.
109. *Accuracy in Media Report*, November, 1988.
110. Lamson, 191.
111. Chesterton, 85.

CHAPTER 4: A PURLOINED CONSCIENCE

1. "Here lies a shadow, ashes, nothing."
2. Hilaire Belloc, *Notes of a Curmudgeon*, (London: Albright's Ltd., 1956), 126.
3. G.K. Chesterton, *Robert Browning*, (London: Macmillan Co., 1914), 93.
4. Peggy Lamson, *Roger Baldwin: Founder of the American Civil Liberties Union*, (Boston: Houghton Mifflin, 1976), 1.
5. Ibid, vii.

6. Ibid, 269.
7. *The Congressional Record*, September 20, 1961.
8. Lamson, 158.
9. William A. Donohue, *The Politics of the American Civil Liberties Union*, (New Brunswick, NJ: Transaction Books, 1985), 45.
10. Lamson, dust-jacket endorsement.
11. William H. McIlhany, *The ACLU on Trial*, (New Rochelle, NY: Arlington House, 1976), 16.
12. Lamson, 2.
13. Ibid, 9.
14. Lamson, 6.
15. Ibid, 2.
16. Ibid, 51.
17. For more on the life, career, and beliefs of Margaret Sanger, see, George Grant, *Grand Illusions: The Legacy of Planned Parenthood*, (Brentwood, TN: Wolgemuth and Hyatt, 1988).
18. Lamson, 62.
19. Ibid, 72.
20. Ibid, 94.
21. Ibid, 117.
22. Ibid, 121.
23. Ibid, 120.
24. Donohue, 31.
25. Lamson, 138–139.
26. Ibid, 141.
27. Roger Baldwin, *Liberty Under the Soviets*, (New York: Vanguard Press, 1928), 8–9.
28. Ibid, 10.
29. Ibid.
30. Ibid.
31. *Soviet Russia Today*, September, 1934.
32. Lamson, 195.
33. *The Review of the News*, August 13, 1975.
34. *Investigation of Communist Propaganda*, House Report 2290, January 17, 1931, 56–57.
35. Donohue, 4.
36. Ibid.
37. *News and Views*, September, 1957.
38. *The Review of the News*, August 13, 1975.
39. Lamson, 188.

40. Jon Winokur, *The Portable Curmudgeon*, (New York: New American Library, 1987), 170.

41. *The Review of the News*, August 13, 1975.

42. Winokur, 92.

43. Theodore Roosevelt, *The Foes of Our Own Household*, (New York: Charles Scribner's Sons, 1917, 1926), 103.

CHAPTER 5: RELIGIOUS EXPRESSION

1. Hilaire Belloc, *The Path to Rome*, (New York: Penguin Books, 1958), 126–127.

2. G.K. Chesterton, *Conversion*, (New York: Macmillan Co., 1951), 86.

3. "He who trifles in the pulpit shall weep in hell."

4. Hilaire Belloc, *The Servile State*, (London: T.N. Foulis, 1913), 148.

5. G.K. Chesterton, *Lunacy and Letters*, (New York: Sheed and Ward, 1958), 191.

6. *Policy Review*, September, 1988.

7. *ACLU Policy Guide*, 159–190.

8. *The Boston Herald*, April 6, 1988.

9. *Policy Review*, September, 1988.

10. Ibid.

11. Ibid.

12. *Imprimis*, April, 1983.

13. Joseph Story, *Commentaries on the Constitution*, (New York: John A. Tallirude and Sons, 1833, 1967), 161–162.

14. *Zorach v. Clausen*, (343 U.S. 306), 1952.

15. Ibid.

16. Walker P. Whitman, *A Christain History of the American Republic: A Textbook for Secondary Schools*, (Boston: Green Leaf Press, 1939, 1948), 42.

17. Robert Ferrell, *The Adams Family: Four Generations of Patriots*, (New York: Publius Press, 1969), 12.

18. Whitman, 91.

19. Ibid, 97.

20. Alfred G. Knophler, *The Lessons of Southern Culture*, (Atlanta: Jefferson Davis Publishers, 1977), 33.

21. Harold K. Lane, *Liberty! Cry Liberty!* (Boston: Lamb and Lamb Tractarian Society, 1939), 31.

22. Whitman, 109.

23. Lane, 32.

24. Geoff Archer, *The War Between the States and its Aftermath*, (Philadelphia: Everson College Press, 1959), 72–73.

25. Theodore Roosevelt, *The Foes of Our Own Household*, (New York: Charles Scribner's Sons, 1917, 1926), 134.

26. Gary DeMar, *Ruler of the Nations: Biblical Principles for Government*, (Fort Worth, TX: Dominion Press, 1987), 232.

27. *Imprimis*, April, 1983.

28. Quoted in Roosevelt, 3; 133.

CHAPTER 6: ABORTION, INFANTICIDE, AND EUTHANASIA

1. "Here the devil shows himself."

2. Hilaire Belloc, *The Path to Rome*, (New York: Penguin Books, 1958), 93.

3. G.K. Chesterton, *Orthodoxy*, (New York: Dodd, Mead, and Company, 1908), 39–40.

4. Janet Benshoof et al., *Preserving the Right to Choose*, (New York: ACLU Reproductive Freedom Project, 1986).

5. William A. Donohue, *The Politics of the American Civil Liberties Union*, (New Brunswick, NJ: Transaction Books, 1985), 102.

6. *ACLU Policy Guide*, 345–348.

7. Ibid, 361.

8. *ACLU Annual Report*, 1986–1987, 27.

9. Ibid.

10. *ACLU Policy Guide*, 345.

11. Quotes taken from Hugo Adam Bedau, *The Case Against the Death Penalty*, (New York: ACLU, 1984), 2.

12. Ibid, 3.

13. Ibid, 3–4.

14. Ibid, 4.

15. *ACLU Policy Guide*, 345–348; 361; Benshoof, 3–50; and, Lynn Paltrow et al., *Parental Notice Laws*, (New York: ACLU Reproductive Freedom Project, 1986), 1–28.

16. Benshoof, 5, 18–22; and, *ACLU Policy Guide*, 87.

17. Benshoof, 11, 13, 16–17; and, *ACLU Policy Guide*, 334–342.

18. Benshoof, 13–14; *ACLU Policy Guide*, 87.

19. *Butler Eagle*, September 28, 1970; and *Operation Rescue News Briefs*, March, 1989.

20. Thomas Paine, *Common Sense and Other Essays*, (New York: Signet Classics, 1977), 19.
21. Harold K. Lane, *Liberty! Cry Liberty!* (Boston: Lamb and Lamb Tractarian Society, 1939), 31.
22. Abraham Lincoln, *Speeches, Letters, and Papers: 1860–1864*, (Washington, DC: Capitol Library, 1951), 341–342.
23. Ronald Reagan, *Abortion and the Conscience of a Nation*, (Nashville, TN: Thomas Nelson, 1984), 15.
24. Ibid, 16.
25. Ibid, 18.
26. Quoted in, John W. Whitehead, *The Separation Illusion*, (Milford, MI: Mott Media, 1977), 21.
27. Theodore Roosevelt, *Foes of Our Own Household*, (New York: Charles Scribner's Sons, 1917, 1926), 3.
28. Quoted in, Daniel L. Dreisbach, *Real Threat and Mere Shadow: Religious Liberty and the First Amendment*, (Westchester, IL: Crossway Books, 1987), 19.

CHAPTER 7: PORNOGRAPHY AND PERVERSION

1. "The whole law of piety is still in force."
2. Hilaire Belloc, *The Servile State*, (London: T.N. Foulis, 1913), 58.
3. G.K. Chesterton, *Robert Browning*, (London: Macmillan Co., 1914), 174.
4. Jerry Kirk, *The Mind Polluters*, (Nashville, TN: Thomas Nelson, 1985), 34–35.
5. Reid Carpenter, *Pittsburgh Leadership Foundation*, (Pittsburgh, PA: Pittsburgh Leadership Foundation, 1988), 19.
6. *Report of the Attorney General on Pornography*, (Nashville, TN: Rutlidge Hill Press, 1986).
7. See Carol Tavris and Susan Sadd, *The Redbook Report on Female Sexuality*, (New York: Delacorte Press, 1977).
8. "America In the Eighties," R.H. Bruskin Associates Market Research, 1985.
9. See David Chilton, *Power in the Blood: A Christian Response to AIDS*, (Brentwood, TN: Wolgemuth and Hyatt, Publishers, 1987).
10. See Enrique Rueda and Michael Schwartz, *Gays, AIDS, and You*, (Washington, DC: Free Congress Foundation, 1987).
11. See Walter Evans, *The Bordellos of Nevada*, (Reno, NV: Desert Visitor Press, 1979).

12. *Statistical Abstract of the United States*, (Washington, DC: Bureau of the Census, 1987).

13. Ibid.

14. *New York Newsday*, February 2, 1988.

15. Ibid.

16. *ACLU Policy Guide*, 6–9, 39–40, 260–261, 345–350, 354–357.

17. Shelby M. Harrison and F. Emmerson Andrews, *American Foundations for Social Welfare*, (New York: Russell Sage Foundation, n.d.), 162–163.

18. See E. Carrington Boggin, et al., *The Rights of Gay People: An American Civil Liberties Union Handbook*, (New York: Bantam Books, 1983).

19. See *ACLU Annual Report, 1986–1987*.

20. *Fort Lauderdale News-Sentenal*, May 14, 1989.

21. Ibid.

22. Norman Dorsen, ed., *Our Endangered Rights: The ACLU Report on Civil Liberties Today*, (New York: Pantheon Books, 1984), x.

23. Ibid, xi.

24. Ibid.

25. *The Boston Globe*, August 26, 1977.

26. Quoted in *The Christian News-Observer*, Spring 1988.

27. See Gary Amos, *Defending the Declaration: How the Bible and Christianity Influenced the Writing of the Declaration of Independence*, (Brentwood, TN: Wolgemuth and Hyatt, Publishers, 1989).

28. See Charles S. Hyneman and Donald Lutz, eds., *American Political Writing During the Founding Era, 1760–1805*, (Indianapolis, IN: Liberty Press, 1983).

29. See Herbert W. Titus and Gerald R. Thompson, *America's Heritage: Constitutional Liberty*, unpublished class syllabus, CBN University School of Law, 1988.

30. See Tim LaHaye, *Faith of Our Founding Fathers*, (Brentwood, TN: Wolgemuth and Hyatt, Publishers, 1987).

31. See John W. Whitehead, *The Separation Illusion*, (Milford, MI: Mott Media, 1977).

32. See Gardiner Spring, *The Obligations of the World to the Bible: A Series of Lectures to Young Men*, (New York: Taylor and Dodd, 1839), 95–98.

33. Robert Goguet, *The Origin of Laws*, (New York: John S. Taylor, Publisher, 1821), 302.

34. Ibid, 99.

35. Quoted in the editor's preface to Cotton Mather, *Essays to Do Good*, (Boston: Massachusetts Sabbath School Society, 1845), iv.
36. Harold K. Lane, *Liberty! Cry Liberty!* (Boston: Lamb and Lamb Tractarian Society, 1939), 32–33.
37. Alexis de Toqueville, *Democracy in America*, (New York: Brandt Textbook Publishers, 1966), xvi.
38. Spring, 101–102.
39. Aleksandr Solzhenitsyn, *A Warning to the West*, (New York: Harper and Row, 1978), 64.
40. *ACLU Annual Report 1986–1987*, 10.
41. Spring, 98.

CHAPTER 8: CRIME AND PUNISHMENT

1. "Without Christ, all virtue is worthless."
2. Hilaire Belloc, *The Path to Rome*, (New York: Penguin Books, 1958), 159.
3. G.K. Chesterton, *Fancies Versus Fads*, (New York: Dodd, Mead, and Company, 1923), 55.
4. Charles E. Silberman, *Criminal Violence, Criminal Justice*, (New York: Vintage Books, 1980), 4.
5. Arnold Green, *Crime Abstract: 1976–1986*, (Tulsa, OK: Citizens' Watch Publications, 1987), 11.
6. Silberman, 4.
7. Rus Walton, *Biblical Solutions to Contemporary Problems: A Handbook*, (Brentwood, TN: Wolgemuth and Hyatt, Publishers, 1988), 34.
8. Silberman, 8.
9. Ibid, 6.
10. Cited in *USA Today*, March 9, 1987.
11. Ibid.
12. Charles Colson and Daniel Van Ness, *Convicted: New Hope for Ending America's Crime Crisis*, (Westchester, IL: Crossway Books, 1989), 29.
13. Walton, 59.
14. Green, 16.
15. Silberman, 65.
16. Ibid.
17. Ibid, 67.
18. Green, 16.

19. Walton, 61.
20. *ACLU Policy Guide*, 95–96, 245–263, 269–302, 304–309, 359–360.
21. Ibid.
22. See William A. Donohue, *The Politics of the American Civil Liberties Union*, (New Brunswick, NJ: Transaction Books, 1985), 257–271.
23. *Insight Magazine*, April 17, 1989.
24. Donohue, 258.
25. Ibid.
26. See for example, Charles S. Hyneman and Donald Lutz, *American Political Writing During the Founding Era: 1760–1805*, (Indianapolis, IN: Liberty Press, 1983); as well as Gary North, *Victim's Rights: A Biblical View*, (Tyler, TX: Institute for Christian Economics, 1989).
27. Quoted in Hyneman and Lutz, 234.
28. Ibid.
29. Ibid.
30. Gardiner Spring, *The Obligations of the World to the Bible*, (New York: Taylor and Dodd, 1839), 190.
31. Nathaniel Niles, *Two Discourses on Liberty*, (Newburyport, MS: Albert Cass, Booksellers, 1774), 13–14.
32. Hyneman and Lutz, 692.
33. Josiah Leeds, *Our System of Justice*, (New York: A.S. Barnes and Company, 1879), 38–42.
34. Ibid, 43–46.
35. Colson and Van Ness, 12.
36. Ibid, 29.
37. Ibid.
38. Quoted in, *The Christian Observer*, July, 1986.
39. Colson and Van Ness, 50–51.
40. Cotton Mather, *Essays: To Do Good*, (Boston: Massachusetts Sabbath School Society, 1710, 1845), 44–45.

CHAPTER 9: WHAT THE WORLD NEEDS NOW

1. Hilaire Belloc, *The Path to Rome*, (New York: Penguin Books, 1958), 34.
2. G.K. Chesterton, *All Things Considered*, (New York: Sheed and Ward, 1956), 195.
3. "The cure of diseases."
4. Belloc, 200.

5. G.K. Chesterton, *Orthodoxy*, (New York: Dodd, Mead, and Company, 1908), 30.

6. Quoted by Robert W. Lee, "What the ACLU Represents," *Conservative Digest*, December, 1988, 60.

7. Alvin Toffler, *Future Shock*, (New York: Bantam, 1971), 158.

8. E. F. Schumacher, *Small Is Beautiful*, (New York: Harper and Row, 1975), 52.

9. James Sire, *How to Read Slowly*, (Wheaton, IL: Harold Shaw Publishers, 1978, 1989), 14–15.

10. Paul Johnson, Intellectuals, (New York: Harper and Row, 1989), 1–2.

11. Francis A. Schaeffer, *A Christian Manifesto*, (Westchester, IL: Crossway Books, 1981), 24.

12. Aleksandr I. Solzhenitsyn, *A World Split Apart*, (New York: Harper and Row, 1978), 47–49.

13. For more on this structure and its Scriptural exposition, see: Meredith Kline, *Treaty of the Great King: The Covenant Structure of Deuteronomy*, (Grand Rapids, MI: Wm. B. Eerdman's Publishing Company, 1963); and, Ray R. Sutton, *That You May Prosper: Dominion By Covenant*, (Ft. Worth, TX: Dominion Press, 1987).

14. William A. Donohue, *The Politics of the American Civil Liberties Union*, (New Brunswick, NJ: Transaction Books, 1985), 13.

15. Ibid.

16. Charles Dickens, *A Tale of Two Cities*, (London: Penguin Classics, 1859, 1970), 35.

17. Ibid.

18. This bit of esoterica is not an obscure lesson in botany, but in semiotics. See, Umberto Eco, *The Open Work* (Cambridge, MA: Harvard University Press, 1988).

19. *American Heritage*, August, 1989.

20. Ibid.

21. See Tim LaHaye, *Faith of Our Founding Fathers*, (Brentwood, TN: Wolgemuth and Hyatt, Publishers), 1987; Marshall Foster and Mary Elaine Swanson, *The American Covenant*, (Medford, OR: The Mayflower Institute, 1983); and, Franklin P. Cole, *They Preached Liberty*, (Indianapolis, IN: Liberty Press, 1981).

22. See Francois Furet and Denis Richet, *The French Revolution*, (New York: Macmillan, 1970); James H. Billington, *Fire in the Minds of Men*, (New York: Basic Books, 1980); John Adams, *Discourses on Davila*, (Boston: American Primary Texts, 1790,

1936); Edmund Burke, *Reflections on the Revolution in France*, (New York: Paperbound Classics, 1792, 1958); and, Alexander Hamilton, *The Cause of France*, (New York: E. M. Farber and Sons, 1793, 1899).

23. Quoted from: Henry Cabot Lodge, *Alexander Hamilton*, (New York: Charles Scribner's Sons, 1899, 1922), 253–254.

24. *The World and I*, July, 1989.

25. Corneluis Van Til, *Defense of the Faith*, (Phillipsburg, NJ: Presbyterian and Reformed, 1971), 8.

26. See Richard M. Weaver, *Ideas Have Consequences*, (Chicago: University of Chicago Press, 1948).

27. See Francis A. Schaeffer, *A Christian Manifesto*, (Westchester, IL: Crossway Books, 1981).

28. See Robert Nisbet, *The History of the Idea of Progress*, (New York: Basic Books, 1980).

29. Quoted in Lamar P. Poirot, *The Adams Family: Four Generations of Service*, (Quincy, MA: Truther and Forbes, Publishers, 1921), 109.

CHAPTER 10: REPAIRERS OF THE BREACH

1. "Deeds of the saints."

2. Hilaire Belloc, *The Path to Rome*, (New York: Penguin Books, 1958), 183.

3. G.K. Chesterton, *The Everlasting Man*, (New York: Dodd, Mead, and Compány, 1925), 50.

4. Quoted in Theodore Roosevelt, *The Foes of Our Own Household*, (New York: Charles Scribner's Sons, 1917, 1926), 132.

5. James Carter Braxton, *Gouverneur Morris: A Biographical Sketch*, (Charleston, SC: Braden-Lowell Press, 1911), 99.

6. M.E. Bradford, *A Worthy Company*, (Marlborough, NH: Plymouth Rock Foundation, 1982), 91.

7. Tim LaHaye, *Faith of Our Founding Fathers*, (Brentwood, TN: Wolgemuth and Hyatt, 1987), 133.

8. Braxton, 101.

9. Hans Bruchner, *The Dawning of Darkness: An Eyewitness Account of the Soviet Debacle*, (Los Angeles: Freedom's Light Publications, 1959), 97.

10. Ibid, 99.

11. Morgan Fraser, *Sermons, Discourses, and Essays*, (New York: Braun and Cie, 1799, 1921), 63.

12. Harold K. Lane, *Liberty! Cry Liberty!* (Boston: Lamb and Lamb Tractarian Society, 1939), 33.
13. *The Confession of Faith of the Presbyterian Church,* (Richmond, VA: John Knox Press, 1646, 1861, 1944), 387.
14. George Washington, *Programs and Papers,* (Washington, DC: U.S. George Washington Bicentennial Commission, 1932), 33.
15. Evan Davis, *Our Greatest President,* (New York: Bedford Company, Publishers, 1891), 361.
16. Davis, 366.

APPENDIX A: TAKING ACTION

1. "Let my wealth consist in good works."
2. William H. Covert, *The Changing American Court System,* (Los Angeles: Donneley Press, 1959), 31.
3. Ibid, 43. There is some controversy within Christian academia over the theological orientation of both the Constitution and the Declaration. Some say—with substantial evidence—that the documents are little more than the codification of the principles of Conspiratorial Freemasonry and the European Enlightenment. Others say—again with some very real force—that they are thoroughly entrenched in orthodox and reformed Christianity. For the sake of this book, I am assuming that regardless of the conspiratorial intentions of various founders who were informed by Freemasonry, the Enlightenment, Deism, or Illuminatism, the interpretive grid of the citizenry at large was informed at the very least by a Christian memory. Thus I would concur with the Court's finding in this case.
4. Ibid, 51.
5. Ibid.
6. Ibid, 67.
7. Ibid, 69.
8. Ibid, 74.
9. Ibid, 86.
10. See Richard Neely, *How the Courts Govern America,* (New Haven, CT: Yale University Press, 1981).
11. For details on how this is done and why from a Biblical perspective see my handbook on the subject, *The Changing of the Guard: Biblical Principles of Political Action,* (Fort Worth, TX: Dominion Press, 1987).

12. See Article III, Section 2, Clause 2. For commentary on this little used, but entirely valid legislative tactic, see *Remnant Review*, July 7, 1989, (P.O. Box 8204, Ft. Worth, TX 76124).

APPENDIX B: ACLU FACTS

1. "Holy wisdom."

APPENDIX C: ORGANIZATIONAL RESOURCES

1. "Good deeds."

APPENDIX D: BIBLIOGRAPHIC RESOURCES

1. "Doer of good."

ABOUT THE AUTHOR

George Grant has been a leader in the pro-life movement as well as an advocate for the poor and homeless for more than a decade. He is a well-known, dynamic speaker and the author of seven books, including *In the Shadow of Plenty; The Dispossessed; The Changing of the Guard; A Christian Response to Dungeons and Dragons (with Peter Leithart); Grand Illusions; To the Work;* and *Bringing in the Sheaves.*

Mr. Grant is currently the Minister of Community Services at Coral Ridge Presbyterian Church in Fort Lauderdale, Florida.

The typeface for the text of this book is *Goudy Old Style*. Its creator, Frederic W. Goudy, was commissioned by American Type Founders Company to design a new Roman type face. Completed in 1915 and named Goudy Old Style, it was an instant bestseller. However, its designer had sold the design outright to the foundry, so when it became evident that additional versions would be needed to complete the family, the work was done by the foundry's own designer, Morris Benton. From the original design came seven additional weights and variants, all of which sold in great quantity. However, Goudy himself received no additional compensation for them. He later recounted a visit to the foundry with a group of printers, during which the guide stopped at one of the busy casting machines and stated, "Here's where Goudy goes down to posterity, while American Type Founders Company goes down to prosperity."

Substantive Editing:
Michael S. Hyatt

Copy Editing:
Russell A. Sorensen

Cover Design:
Kent Puckett Associates, Atlanta, Georgia

Page Composition:
Xerox Ventura Publisher
Printware 720 IQ Laser Printer

Printing and Binding:
Maple-Vail Book Manufacturing Group,
York, Pennsylvania

Cover Printing:
Strine Printing
York, Pennsylvania

DATE DUE
